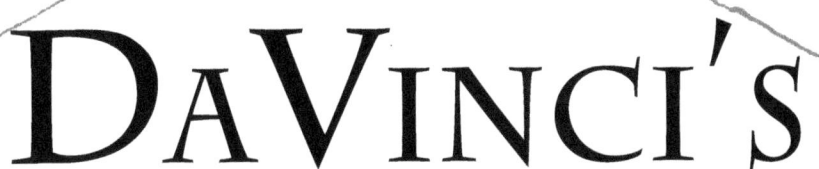

DaVinci's
9
Values

*Revolutionize your painting with
the new "Neutral Near-Blacks"*

W. P. Arteno

ISBN: 9781941138786
Library of Congress Control Number: 2016947949

www.StudioArteno.com

1st Edition, 2016 | Printed in the USA
Three Knolls Publishing | Tucson, Az

Forward

There is usually more than a single purpose for the existence of any particular object. The reason or purpose attributed to the object can often be misleading or misunderstood.

Take for example the chicken egg. It is sometimes used in cooking, either the entire egg, the white portion or just the egg yolk. And although generally intended to be a foodstuff, the egg yolk also happens to be a natural catalyst for the mixing of oil and water, which are ingredients often used together in cooking. In fact, if one should want to enter the realm of Egg Tempera Painting, one should pay homage to the humble egg. For it is the egg that makes tempera painting possible.

Then too, there is the hog bristle paintbrush used by the fine art oil painter. It is much more than just a run-of-the-mill paint brush. First of all, it is made with the very best of bristles obtained only in China. Bristles that have the most desirable curves and length that allow for the most perfectly desired interlocking points. That is to say, an abundance of flags, or split-ends on the tip of each bristle. Flags that lock together to carry the thick or heavy oil paints used in the process of fine art painting.

Finally, let us give some thought to something we should all understand as an artist, an item known as OIL PAINT. When one works with paint, certain alterations can be made that can be considered somewhat normal. For instance, paint can appear to be lighter by adding a white paint. By adding one of the conventional tube blacks, we should get a neutral gray value, but usually, this dark gray change is not quite right.

Sometimes we get a cool or warm temperature from the black color involved. Or we can too often be bothered by the excess employed of oil needed to manufacture the carbon black paint in use.

Each new batch of black is manufactured with a pigment made from a different mix of various materials. Each of the carbon tubes of blacks include: Lamp Black, Ivory or Bone Black, and Vine or Charcoal Black. Even the Black Oxide or Ferric Oxide Mars Black will be altered and different. Regardless which black the artist encounters, a new learning process is required for each.

HAVE NO FEAR! You now hold in your hands the solution to eliminating many problems generated by the four black tube colors. Many artists have dealt with these issues for over seven hundred years. Your author was first introduced to painting over seventy years ago and dealt with the conventional black paint for the first forty years of that time. For the past thirty years, after developing his near-black paints explained in this book, he has painted exclusively with the aforementioned ARTENO'S NEAR-BLACK PAINT with great success.

And now, you can too!.

Walter P. Arteno
March 2016

"He only moves toward the perfection of his art whose criticism surpasses his achievement."
—Leonardo DaVinci

This book is dedicated to those who appreciate the fine art of painting and who accept the humble comment of DaVinci. And to my friends Ingred Williams, Annie Hahn and Meaghan Herdina who contributed much to the completion of this project.

Contents

List of Plates and Charts

First Choice Of Many To Come
Vocabulary
Color Properties

As long ago as 1672, Charles Lebrun, Director of the French Academy of Art, attempted to set forth a disparity between drawing and color with the thought provoking, albeit debatable, statement quoted above. And now, some three hundred years later, a similar rationale of diverse opinion exists.

There are those among us who maintain that the application of color is really an extension of drawing. Others contend that a keen understanding of drawing and a thorough knowledge of color are two separate, although equally complex, unrelated disciplines. Ironically, one of the two concepts can be considered valid or invalid as a given situation might dictate.

What is the key? In what context or format are these two different pursuits being employed?

Let us consider the "extension of drawing"

concept. One might argue that many of the same basic rules or cannons required of conventional drawing can also apply to the application of color, particularly in representational or figurative works of art. Many of the various concepts employed to render three-dimensional illusions, are as such: the source or direction of light, brilliance or intensity of color purity, value or degree of color grayness, simulated atmospheric conditions, controlled haloing and desired fuzziness or vagueness. They can all, at times, be applied to both conventional drawing as well as abstract color application. Be it landscape, seascape, portrait, genre or still life rendering, the same rationale can be applied to the 'extension of drawing' concept.

However, the opposing argument or "separate discipline" concept can also be compelling. Many times one might see color employed in an abstract art form. That is to say, with little or no reference to conventional realism, neither figurative nor representational, and sometimes devoid of many basic drawing concepts.

The innate power of color often stands on its own merits as a recognized independent force in the visual arts. Furthermore, a comprehensive knowledge of the many complex aspects of color: the science of color, the psychological or emotional approach to color, as well as the difficulties encountered in color manipulation, also lends credence to the argument that color and the application of color can legitimately be considered a valid and separate discipline.

Perhaps the most compelling case for either or both sides of the debate is grounded in virtual reality. The reality that there are those artists, both past and present, who prefer one concept over the other, and whose preference is clearly apparent in their art work, and work habits.

Although there have been numerous attempts to categorize the many different techniques or styles of various painters in general, it is reasonable to say that they fall mostly into two broad categories: the realist versus the abstract artist. Therefore, a word of warning is in order. Beware the term 'abstract art' as it can mean many things to many people.

There is in addition a third group, somewhat more difficult to classify, because their work is not as easily discernible. This group's work falls somewhere between realism and abstract. Any semblance of previously conceived drawing is done with the brush directly on the picture plane and becomes an integral part of the finished product. It is an extremely difficult technique to master, known as the direct method or *alla prima* painting. For that reason, although a form of drawing, it can also be considered somewhat abstract.

For example, the work of Flemish born artist, Frans Hals, circa 1581-1666, has been described as "one of the inexplicable miracles" of Dutch painting. His portrait painting, *The Laughing Cavalier,* (1624), is an excellent example of the direct technique, with his spontaneity, and unerring control. No known drawings by Hals are thought to exist, and there is every indication his approach was *alla prima*. When his work is observed close-up, his freehand style looks haphazard. But at a distance his paintings are beautiful examples of combining drawing and color as if an integral whole.

Of the two extremes, let us first consider the realistic paintings of Jacob Van Ruisdael (1628-1682) and Jean Auguste Dominique Ingres (1780-1867). One need only observe Ruisdael's two paintings of the same subject, the *Dresden Jewish Cemetery* and the *Detroit Jewish Cemetery*, compared to his drawing entitled *Tombs In The Jewish Cemetery At Outerkerk* to realize the correlation between conventional drawing and color application. The ability to render detail, to record exactitude, and capture a mood are all elements of good drawing, regardless of the medium employed.

A like conclusion can be attained by examining the delicacy rendered in both the preliminary pencil drawings and subsequent portrait paintings by Ingres. Perhaps the most compelling case for the "painting as an extension of drawing" argument, are the very words of Ingres himself. He once stated, "An artist can learn all there is to know about color in an afternoon". Could it be he considered drawing the more complex or difficult aspect of the two disciplines? He also said, "Drawing is the probity of art", which can easily be translated to mean, all the goodness and virtue of art can be attributed to drawing. At any rate, it is quite possible that both Ruisdael and Ingres subscribed to the principle that drawing took precedence to the application of color.

None made a point more succinctly than Paul Cezanne (1839-1906) when he said, "Drawing and color are by no means two different things. As you paint, you draw."

It should be noted that, in varying degrees, this general attitude concerning color as an extension of drawing prevailed in the western art world for centuries. It began as early as the fifteenth century and continued on until the latter part of the nineteenth century.

At that time the intrinsic strength and beauty of color, together with the emotions color can provoke, came to the fore. Granted, it was a slow process, but eventually the art world began accepting color for color's sake without the assistance or necessity of realistic representation to make it a force in the visual arts.

Events in the art world of the twentieth century radically affected the Renaissance domination of both lineal and color perspective. However, the fact that color has become such an important and independent element in much of today's art, does if, in no way, subordinate the relevance of drawing. Nor does it diminish the importance of good design.

Now let us consider the opposite extreme:

the argument that drawing and a knowledge of color and color application are separate disciplines. Are they really two different media independent of one another?

The idea that one can create a work of art with color alone, without the aid of drawing, is perhaps within the realm of possibility. But to contend that all abstract art supports the argument is a mistaken generalization fraught with misunderstandings or misconceptions. It warrants a word of judgmental caution. Be aware of the inordinate amount of generalized supposition on the part of the general public, as well as the many and varied theories postulated by the artists involved.

Too often the term "abstract art" is misconstrued. It is as if the two words are at variance with each other and the term is something of an enigma. For centuries the word "art" implied the physical, tangible, recognizable representation of reality. Whereas the word "abstract" dealt with thought, theory, emotional subjectivity, non-representational, and in some instances, to extract or remove from reality. Consequently, when the two words are combined, they can lead to conceptual variation. In actuality the term "abstract art" means different things to different people. The term does not denote a particular movement, but rather a general attitude that rejected much that dealt with both social and aesthetic principles.

Even the manner in which the entire

abstract art process evolved was one of complexities and contention. It had its start in Europe just prior to, or early in, the twentieth century and took hold in the United States somewhat later. It evolved during a century fraught with two world wars, an industrial revolution, a universal depression, extreme labor unrest, and considerable social disruption.

It was a time of artistic revolt and a century of many "isms". It began as a rejection of academic doctrine, and the function of color was an *a priori* issue. It was a period that stressed self-awareness, a new way of seeing, and a different interpretation of light and color. A century that stimulated much diversity, both in pictorial renderings and conceptual thinking. Whether the driving force was visceral or cerebral in origin, eventually both intent and style brought about radical aesthetic change. Eventually there was pictorial distortion, the elimination of representational or figurative imagery, and ultimately, an attempt to reject the basic fundamentals of drawing all together.

It was a revolution in artistic rationale that started with Impressionism and heralded the advent of Post Impressionism, Symbolism, Fauvism, Cubism, Orphism, Futurism, Surrealism, Dadaism, Abstract Expressionism and Modernism, to name but a few of the many diversified movements. These were art movements, each with a different agenda. Each intent on challenging one aspect or another of the traditional. But they all had one thing in common: an awareness of the power of color.

There was no stronger advocate of this salient point than Robert Delauney, (1885-1941) a leading advocate of Orphism. An artist who approached the abstract from an intellectual point of view and who once stated, "Color alone is form and subject." Delauney was concerned with the "dynamic energy of light and color contrasts," and explored, "transparency of color whose similarity to musical notes led to discovery of movement in color." And although he was a strong proponent and did much to advance the concept of non-figurative imagery, his highly acclaimed painting *Circular Forms; Sun And Moon,* circa 1912, is nevertheless dependent on basic drawing elements, i.e., perspective, form, and line are all apparent.

The Russian, Wassily Kandinsky, (1866-1944) who, in contrast to Delauney, approached the abstract from a visceral or intuitive position: if it felt right, it is right. He once wrote, "One will never find the possibility to make a painting without color and line, but without object has existed in our time....". And although he eventually developed a more disciplined geometric style, his *Study For Composition No. 7,* (1913) is an example of his early non-objective abstract art, where once again elements of drawing, namely form and depth, are apparent.

Four decades later the American, Jackson Pollock, (1912-1956) "was impressed with the European concept of the source of art being the unconscious." One of his last paintings,

Convergence, (1952) attests to his claim, "My paintings do not have a center, but depend on the same amount of interest throughout." Pollock was an Abstract Impressionist and the creator of the "drip painting." Which is an innovative artistic process executed, according to him, "with no preconceived plan, drawing or color sketches." However, just as line, shape, form and depth, are elements of drawing, rhythm and design are also two very important elements of his work.

No matter which argument one chooses to champion, be it the "separate discipline" or the "extension of drawing," one factor is common to both: an awareness that the mastery of color is an *a priori* issue, requiring a rather high degree of mental discipline and considerable technical knowledge. Regardless which type of painting one chooses to pursue, in addition to a working knowledge of color, there is a possibility one will encounter various aspects of the natural sciences, e.g., physics, chemistry, geology, biology, and botany. And of course, even as a novice, one can expect the need for certain mathematical know how, e.g., angles, ratios, geometry, and so on.

Be it oil or watercolor rendering, egg tempera, a wardrobe color choice, the printing of a magazine, or an interior decorating decision, a thorough knowledge of color is imperative if we are to make an intelligent decision, attain desired success, or refrain from being overwhelmed by the mystic properties of colors. Even the immense number of decisions required in the color manipulation process, both subjective and objective, can be inhibiting.

Therefore, if for no other reason than the anticipated large number of diverse problems one will inevitably encounter, a need for an appropriate, comprehensive, definitive vocabulary is of primary concern. And as an aid to accomplish that objective, note that certain key words, terms, and phrases have been highlighted throughout the text.

Often when one embarks on the study of any subject, one should seek out and develop a relevant, accurate vocabulary. For it is first necessary to master the language, the terminology, the nomenclature, and the idioms of any technical discipline if one desires to adequately comprehend, to be sufficiently analytical, or if one merely desires to acquire additional information concerning any given topic.

Consider, if one were to search the world over, no more then nine colors would be realized. It could be safely assumed that every painting ever completed was accomplished by using some combination of these basic nine colors. But just as in music, many things come to bear on the way to make a mere seven musical notes combine to make music. And so it is with these select colors: many color alterations are possible.

There are only three groups of three, for a total of nine, distinct, diverse and enigmatic colors.

Group one, consists of yellow, blue, and red that constitute the three **primary colors.** They are referred to as primary because they cannot be created by mixing together two or more colors from the various color families.

Group two contains orange, green, and purple which represent the three **secondary colors**, because they can be created by mixing two or more of the primary colors together.

Group three is comprised of the three **non-prismatic** colors known as brown, white, and black. They are considered non-prismatic because they cannot be readily seen or detected when a glass prism is employed to extract the primary and secondary colors from sunlight.

For our purposes, **hue** is a term indicating a modification of a **tube color**, or a color family. Once the **properties of color** have been modified in any manner, we have, in essence, changed the composition of the basic tube color, or it can have reference to a family, say red, of color. Too often, the two terms, color and hue, are often used in place of one another, with little or no consideration of the various color properties involved.

Of these nine different generic color groups, all represent numerous nuanced color variations capable of the extremely pronounced colors to the most delicately subtle colors. And no matter how definitive the various contrasts are, each can be attributed to any one, or more likely a combination of more than one, of the four elusive and often difficult to control properties of color.

PROPERTIES OF COLOR

Value: A term that refers to the degree of how dark or how light a given color appears in terms of gray. That is to say, if one can imagine removing color from color, that which remains is an intrinsic value, from light to dark, underlying each and every conceivable color combination.

Temperature: A term that refers to a concept whereby a given color can be considered either hot or cold, warm or cool, or in rare instances, can reflect a **Neutral Temperature** by theoretically registering no temperature extremes whatever. However, this is a matter of subjective judgment.

Chroma: A term that refers to the intensity of comparative brilliance of an unaltered pure "tube" color; i.e., with no property changes. The pure undiluted color brilliance is known as color **Chroma**. It is also common to qualify various colors in terms of chroma. For instance, yellow is of a much higher chroma than the color blue. But just as with the subjective judgment concerning temperature, all judgment concerning chroma is of a comparative nature, and therefore a somewhat debatable issue.

Sfumata: A term that refers to an implied dusty or smoky quality or property of a color that is generally apparent when the color value and chroma have been altered by the addition of one of the various available white tube colors. Also, a color wherein an **Opaque** paint pigment of a lighter color intensity or chroma is employed to emphasize the dusty or smoky effect.

And it is with these color properties and their reaction to various manipulations and alterations that will be the subject of much of this book.

*"We are therefore justified in concluding that white light
is in reality (color) lights."*
A.P. Lourie
The Painters Methods and Materials

***White Light and Color
Pigment Comments
Refractive Index
Incident Light Ray***

In order that we better understand and
analyze the properties of color, we should first
understand the phenomenon and significance
of daylight, or white light. For both white
light and color collectively emanate from the
sun in the form of **waves of electromagnetic
radiation**. Radiation waves of solar power,
collectively comprised of energy waves
of varying lengths, including radio waves,
ultraviolet waves, X-ray waves, and the
potentially **visible waves** that, subject to certain
ideal conditions, can be made to appear as
illuminating sunlight and possibly select color
variations. So can we not consider, white light is
in fact the very essence of color?

Although these waves travel a distance
of 93,000,000 miles from the sun to earth
at an approximate speed of 186,281 miles

per second, it is somewhat ironic that these electromagnetic visible waves of potential sunlight and latent color collectively make the long journey in total darkness. And not until some manner of measurable **resistance** is encountered, such as generated by the various dense materials of the Earth's outer atmosphere, does a noticeable change occur.

That slight change is brought about by the appropriate type and degree of resistance required to establish a faint glimmer of white light. A subtle glow of sunlight that grows more intense as it encounters additional resistance on its earth-bound journey. And if by chance sufficient moisture is also encountered, i.e., resistance, in the form of rain, it is possible for those visual waves of the newly established sunlight to be altered again and caused to appear as the six separate and distinct colors of Nature's rainbow. See Plate A.

So, armed with a knowledge of these unique energy waves, and an awareness of their potential transformation qualities, i.e., electromagnetic radiation to white light, and white light to color, it is possible to enhance one's ability to manipulate and effectively control both color, and the too often perplexing, properties of color.

For example, consider the various color results one can obtain with the aid of a form of resistance called a **glass prism**. See Plate B, Fig. 1.

If a ray of white light were directed to strike one of the three surfaces of a glass prism

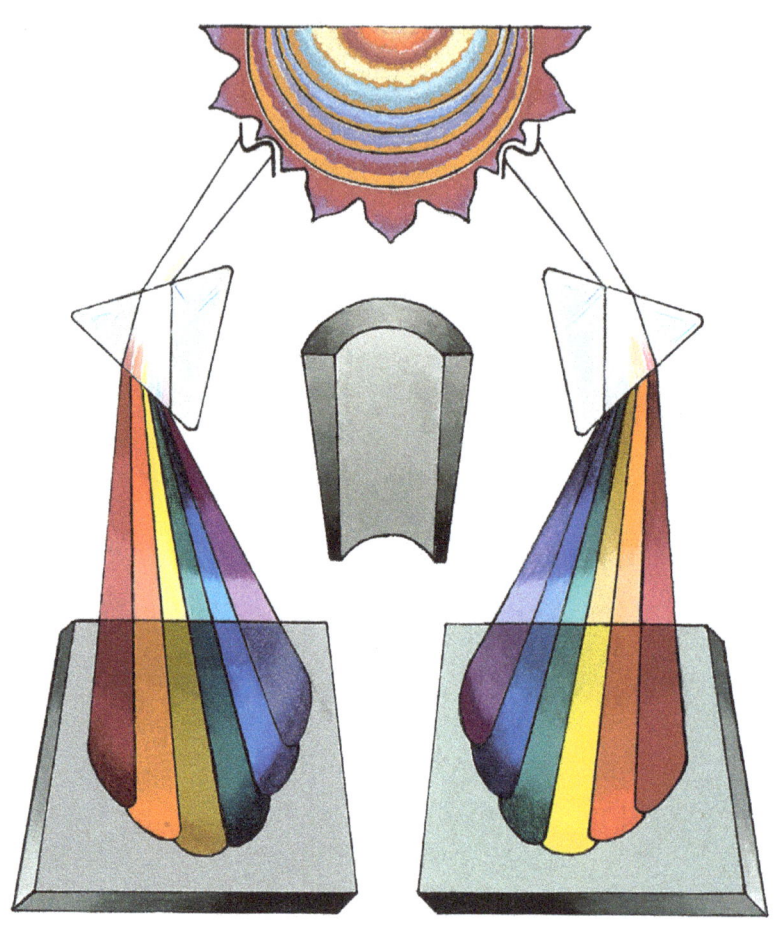

Plate A

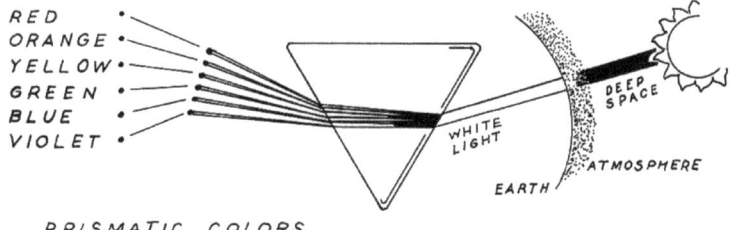

PRISMATIC COLORS

Fig. 1.

· —— — ——— ·

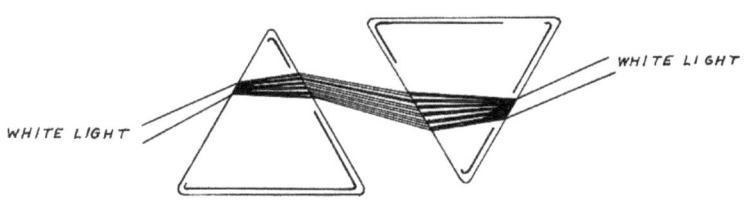

Fig.2.

· —— — — ——— ·

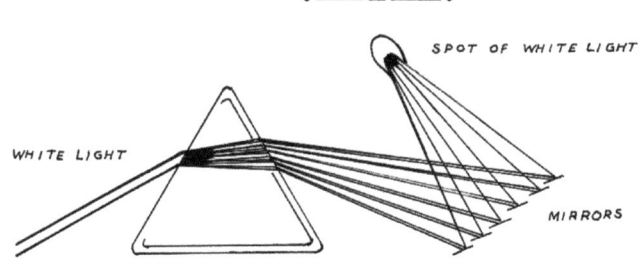

Fig 3.

Plate B

17

at a near ninety degree angle, then depending on the amount of resistance encountered and the degree of the oblique angle of attack involved, the light ray will inevitably bend and change direction and in turn realize a slight reduction in speed. And because of this sudden decline in velocity, coupled with the sequential length variation of the soon to be visible color waves, they will have a tendency to separate, fan-like, and depart the opposing polygonal surface of the prism as rays of **prismatic color**; the same orderly presentation of the six colors or **color spectrum**, displayed by the rainbow.

However, that is only one example of how the prism can be used in the manipulation of color. Consider that with the aid of a second prism, it is possible to reunite the prismatic color generated by the first prism and establish them once again as non-discernible waves of white light. If each individual color ray established by a prism were made to strike an appropriately angled "reflective surface" and caused to converge at a given point, they would once again collectively merge at a spot of white light. See Plate B, Fig 2.

Thus with the aid of the prism, controlled manipulation of both white light and prismatic color can be achieved. However, it is essential to realize that the prism also represents the one indispensable stimulus repeatedly needed to activate each phase of the entire sunlight and prismatic color of the electromagnetic energy conversion process, i.e., the all important constant element of resistance, as emphasized in the following summation.

One: Radiation from the electromagnetic energy that emanates from the sun and journeys through deep space in total darkness until such time that it eventually encounters some form of resistance;

Two: Resistance that triggers the appearance of sunlight. Or more specifically, the white light that continues it's earth-bound journey as the bearer of non-discernible color waves, until such time that it encounters yet another form of resistance;

Three: Resistance that triggers the appearance of the six color variations of the color spectrum. And no matter an act of nature in the form of rain, or an event of applied science in the form of a prism, the **color dispersion reaction** cannot occur with the assistance of yet another appropriate form of resistance;

Four: Resistance that can be made to trigger the return of prismatic color to white light, thus establishing the fact that both white light and color can be made to react and interact one with the other, given the appropriate means of resistance;

Five: Resistance required in an effectively controlled electromagnetic conversion procedure established every time we undertake to manipulate a color or the various properties of color. Although the universally admired color display of the rainbow is most impressive, it remains an uncontrolled event of nature; whereas, those basic materials employed by the would-be-colorist to accomplish a desired color reaction, must of necessity meet certain physical qualifications if the materials involved can be expected to perform in a prescribed manner.

For example, if one should want to extract from white light any singular color or a specific color property, the material or ingredient(s) selected to accomplish the job of resistance, needs to be of a uniform and desirable standard of quality if one is to accomplish the desired results in a predictable manner. Likewise, if one wants to favorably induce the possibility of **light fastness** or **fade resistance** of a particular color, consideration must first be given to the **relative density** inherent in whatever form of resistance that is employed to accomplish the desired result.

All the major ingredients of any paint form should be of paramount concern. Necessity dictates the ability to detect, calibrate, and index even the slightest degree of measurable resistance of any component of paint. This is basic to ones ability to effectively select, manipulate, and control both color and the various properties of any given color. Although this task generally falls to the manufacturers of the various pigments and vehicles that eventually become the colors we, as painters, normally enjoy.

There are times that even a limited

knowledge of the classification procedure or indexing process can be advantageous to both the accomplished, as well as the inexperienced colorist.

No one will ever see white light, color or a rainbow without the necessary required resistance, be it atmospheric air, oil, water, or that which we call a **pigment**. Pigment is the general term we use to identify a substance or material as the name of a specific color, but seldom do we consider the origin, property, or function of the pigment. By now one should realize that the primary purpose of the pigment is to function as a substance of resistance in the conversion process of white light to color.

The author, Ralph Mayer, The Artist's Handbook of Materials and Techniques, lists the "Requirement for a Paint Pigment," of which a partial listing is as follows:

1. Should be a smooth, finely ground powder.

2. Should be insoluble in the medium it is used.

3. Should withstand the action of sunlight without changing color.

4. Should not exert a harmful chemical action upon the medium or upon other pigments with which it is to be mixed.

5. Should be chemically inert and unaffected by materials with which it is to be mixed or by oxidation.

6. Should have the proper degree of opacity or transparency to suit the purpose for which

it is intended.

Again, we cannot forget to always consider the four properties of color: value, temperature, chroma, and sfumata. Add to this the inherent attribute of the pigment to be **Transparent**, **Semi-transparent,** or **Opaque.** Each of these extremely important properties will be discussed later, but first let us concern ourselves with the origin of some of the more common pigments.

Pigments fall into two broad categories of origin. The first is organic, i.e., vegetable or animal. The other is inorganic, i.e., mineral. In either category, organic or inorganic, both natural and artificial pigments can be developed.

As an example, the "lake" pigments are artificially made. **Dyes** are fixed or attached to some form of clear base material. Many of the dyestuffs in use today are made from coal tar, although some are of natural vegetable or animal origin.

Indigo, for instance, is an organic dye made from plant life, while Indian Yellow is made from the urine of a cow that is fed mainly mango leaves. There is an Eurasian herb, the madder plant, from whose roots are extracted a dye known as "aquamarine", the basis for the very popular red paint, Alizarin Crimson.

The "cadmium" pigments are artificially prepared inorganic mineral pigments, and although fairly new, they exhibit outstanding color properties.

And then there are the pigments formed

when certain materials are induced to enter the process of **oxidation**. Rust is a residue **oxide pigment** made by the corrosion of iron. It is interesting to note that hydrated iron oxide will produce a yellow pigment, and if heated to the anhydrous state (moisture removed), the iron oxide will produce a red pigment. Both lead and zinc create a white form of oxidation used to make a very good white paint. With sulfur, a yellow powder occurs, and with copper, there is a green color oxidation material developed.

In the case of black, the pigmentation is generally carbon. The color Lampblack is made from carbon created from burning oil or gas. Charcoal Black is made from burnt vine clippings, and Ivory Black or Bone Black pigments are made by heating ivory or bone fragments.

Then there are the earth pigments. They include Ochre, Sienna, and Umber. They can be roughly described as a clay stained with compounds of iron, and as their names indicate, the latter two were pigments from an area in Italy.

Viridian Green is prepared by heating together potassium dichromate with boric acid and then washing the product. While Cobalt Green is a compound of the oxides of zinc and cobalt with extreme heat applied. The cadmium colors, yellow and orange are sulfides of the metal cadmium, where sulfuric acid is used in the oxidizing process.

The original Ultramarine Blue was extracted from Lapis Lazuli (a semi-precious stone). The stone is ground, heated, and mixed with resin and oil, leaving the mixture for some weeks and then kneading the mass under water rendered slightly alkaline by wood ashes. This was a remarkably permanent blue of a very beautiful quality and rather costly. Today we have artificial blue made by heating together silica soda, sulfur and coal.

Although these are but a few of the numerous available pigments, much can be discerned of their origin and properties.

Pigments can be derived from inert earth to plant roots, from semi-precious stones to burnt oil residue, from the decomposition of minerals, either pure or compound, through an act of nature or with the application of acid. One thing is certain, the human propensity to discover, to alter, to perpetuate pigments has been a significant part of history. They are a form of resistance that has been mined, ground, and washed. They are burnt, roasted, and cooked. They are pulverized, squeezed, and subjected to acids. Moisture is added and moisture is removed. These processes are all undertaken with one objective in mind: to obtain a unique pigment of a specific color or a pigment that will display the desired properties on a near permanent basis. It is important to realize however, that at the time a pigment is integrated with, or immersed in a **vehicle**, which can be as varied as oil, water, or egg yolk, the pigment can no longer be considered a clean pigment, for it is now part of a paint.

While we have established the need for

nature's form of resistance to bring about both daylight and the spectrum of color, there is also a means of resistance whereby a **Refractive index** can be established. See Plate C.

To establish an **Index of Refraction Scale** we start by using a vacuum, as there can be no extraneous element of resistance present that could distort the speed or refraction of the light ray involved. By observing Figure 1, one should note a line runs perpendicular to the **surface of substance** which constitutes a constant. Where the angle of the incident light ray traveling through the vacuum chamber comes into contact with the surface of a substance, a portion of that light becomes a **reflected light ray**. Because of a change in the two different mediums, i.e., vacuum to substance, there is a reduction in speed and refraction of the original light ray. If we consider the constant perpendicular line and new angle of the light ray, an **Angle of Refraction** is established, or a **Refractive Index Number** for each individual type of pigment. Which brings us to the next phase of the light-color relationship, and the importance of the refractive quality of a given pigment particle. See Plate C, Figure 2.

The chart depicts the reaction of light as it encounters a pigment particle suspended in a vehicle, be it water or oil. The function of a pigment, in addition to performing as a specific color, can better be understood if one can envision an **incident-light-ray** encountering the surface of the vehicle and the five step reaction

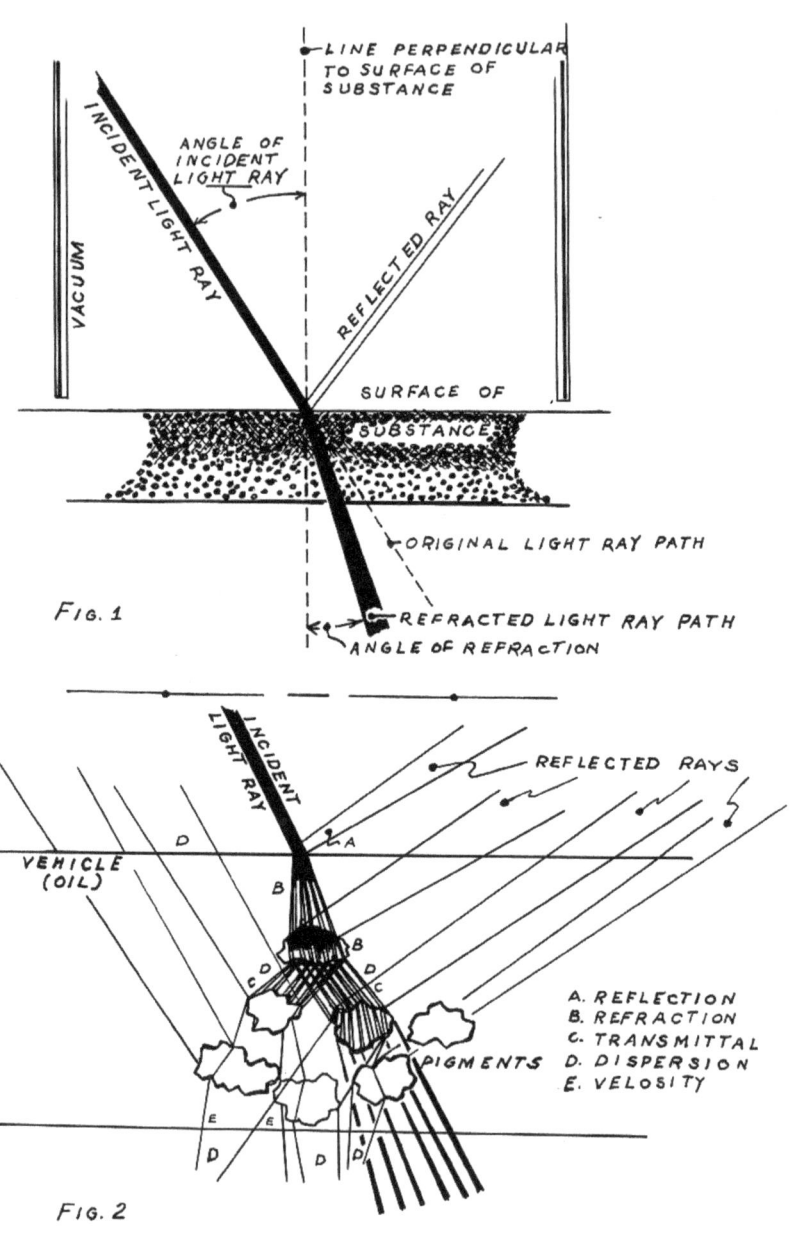

LINE PERPENDICULAR TO SURFACE OF SUBSTANCE

ANGLE OF INCIDENT LIGHT RAY

INCIDENT LIGHT RAY

REFLECTED RAY

VACUUM

SURFACE OF SUBSTANCE

ORIGINAL LIGHT RAY PATH

REFRACTED LIGHT RAY PATH

ANGLE OF REFRACTION

FIG. 1

INCIDENT LIGHT RAY

REFLECTED RAYS

VEHICLE (OIL)

PIGMENTS

A. REFLECTION
B. REFRACTION
C. TRANSMITTAL
D. DISPERSION
E. VELOSITY

FIG. 2

Plate C

that follows:

A. Reflected Light: A portion of an incident light ray, upon contacting the **surface of a vehicle**, such as oil or water, will reflect away from the point of contact. The amount of reflection encountered is determined by the type of vehicle and its index of resistance.

B. Refracted Light: After the light contacts the vehicle and is then reflected, the balance of the light will penetrate the vehicle and encounter a portion of the pigment and once again undergo refraction and then continue its journey.

C. Transmittal: Each time a substance of resistance is encountered, the portion of the light ray not lost through reflection will continue its course of transmittal on a newly altered course at a reduced velocity until it encounters some other particle of pigment.

D. Dispersion: When light rays encounter a substance of obstruction, in addition to bending the light and reducing its velocity, it also causes the light to disperse or spread fan-like. It then continues its progress in similar fashion, over and over. Thus the process continues as long as a portion of the original light ray exists and some degree of velocity remains. However, it should be noted, white light is finite.

E. Velocity: There are many factors that contribute to a reduction of the velocity of the incident light ray. Each aspect of the reflection, refraction, dispersion, and transmittal process can have a diminishing affect on the velocity of the light ray.

Not all objects of obstruction register the same amount of resistance. Some reflect more than others, some permit more *transmittal* than others, and some account for a greater or lesser degree of *refraction* than others. Whichever the cause, the entire *velocity* reduction or absorbent process of the light is directly related to the Index, Refraction, or Resistance encountered.

There are no lines in nature. They are only a device for the artist to indicate a potential change in value.

"There are no lines in nature. They are only a device for the artist to indicate a potential change in value."
The Author

The Dual Color Wheel
Basic Palette
Extended Secondary Color

In his book, <u>The Artists Handbook of Material and Techniques</u>, Ralph Myers compiled a list of four hundred and eighty-two different paint pigments. Of these, he compiled a list of forty-six pigments considered suitable as oil paint pigments. Of these forty-six suitable pigments, we have selected twelve colors to create the Dual Color Wheel, and eventually, to establish a portion of the color palette. See Charts 1 and 1A.

A color wheel is divided into six sections, as indicated by the six pointed star in the center. Three points of the star bear the first letter of each of the generic names of the three primary colors: yellow, red and blue. The other three points indicate the secondary colors: purple, orange and green, for a total of six color divisions. There are also two of each like hues in both primary and secondary colors. Also displayed in each set of colors is a variation of temperature; one color being warm and one color being cool. It is most important to realize that it is the presence of this temperature that generates a major problem when attempting to gray or darken a given color.

The black or gray portion of the star was painted with an unusual type of "black paint" created with a mixture of three different colors: Raw Umber, Ultramarine Violet and Phthalo Green, which can be seen in the Purple Value Variation Chart, mixture four. You will see it at the bottom left of the dual color wheel chart 1A. This particular black is one of twenty-four near-black color mixtures that has cast some doubt on the worth of a conventional color wheel. We will be discussing near-blacks as we proceed.

The three points of the star painted orange, green and purple are pointing to the respective secondary colors that make up a part of the Dual Color Wheel.

As one can see by looking at the top of the Dual Color Wheel, the two yellow colors, Cadmium Yellow Light and Yellow Ochre, are opposite the two purple primary colors, Manganese Violet and Ultramarine Violet. In addition, there are four purple secondary hues made by various controlled mixtures of red and blue. They were composed with Alizarin Crimson, Cadmium Red Deep and either Ultramarine Blue or Phthalo Blue (referenced on the chart as TB). Each color, both yellow and purple, are the complement of one another. See Chart 1A for color application in Chart 1.

To the right of the wheel a similar situation occurs. Directly opposed to the two blue primary colors, Phthalo Blue (TB) and Ultramarine Blue, are Cadmium Red Light and Cadmium Orange. In addition there are four orange secondary hues, made by various controlled mixtures of reds and yellows. They were composed with Yellow Ochre, Alizarin Crimson, Cadmium Yellow Light, and Cadmium Yellow Deep. Here the colors and hues, blue and orange, are complements of one another.

To the left of the color wheel, directly opposed to the two primary colors of red, Alizarin Crimson and Cadmium Red Dark, there are two secondary green colors, Viridian Green and Phthalo Green (TG). There are also four green hues, made by various controlled mixtures of blue and yellow. They are composed of Cadmium Yellow Light, Yellow Ochre and Ultramarine Blue or Phthalo Blue (TB on chart). Therefore, the two colors, red and green, complement one another.

In the prior three paragraphs we have pointed out the two different colors in each of the three primary/secondary groups, and the fact that each of the two colors complement one or the other. They are known as **complements.** When a primary and complementary secondary color are placed side by side, they appear to be more intense or brighter in appearance, and less brilliant when placed in

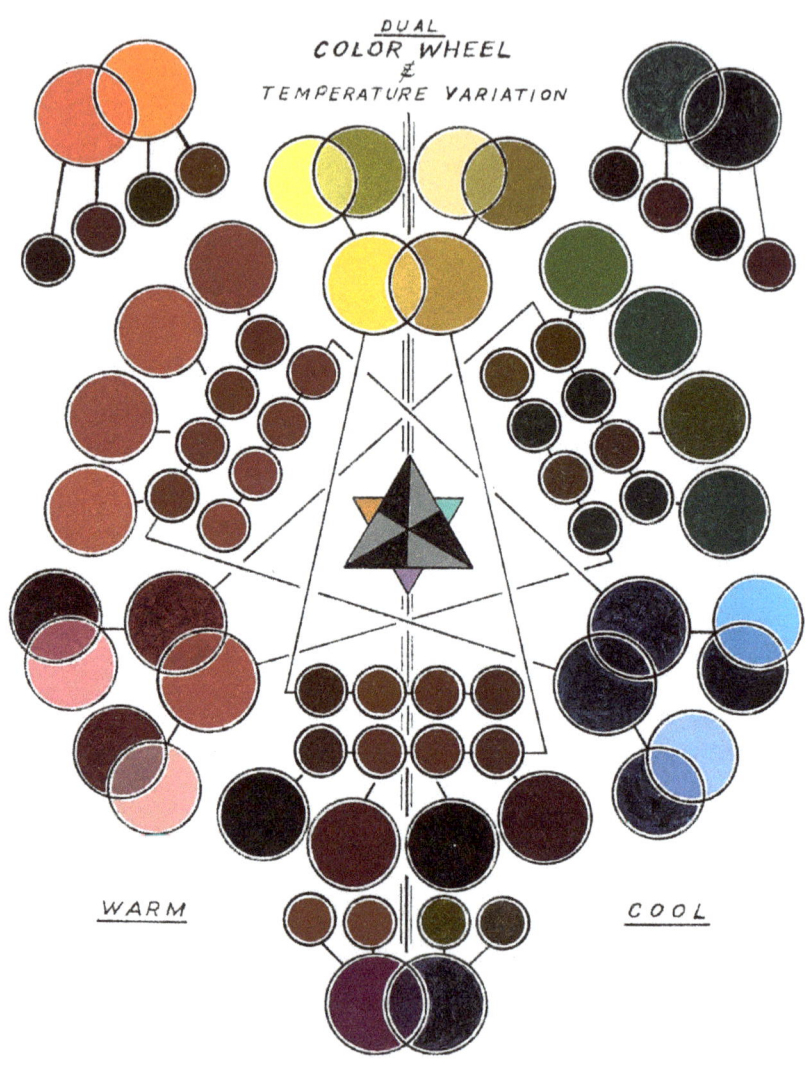

Chart 1

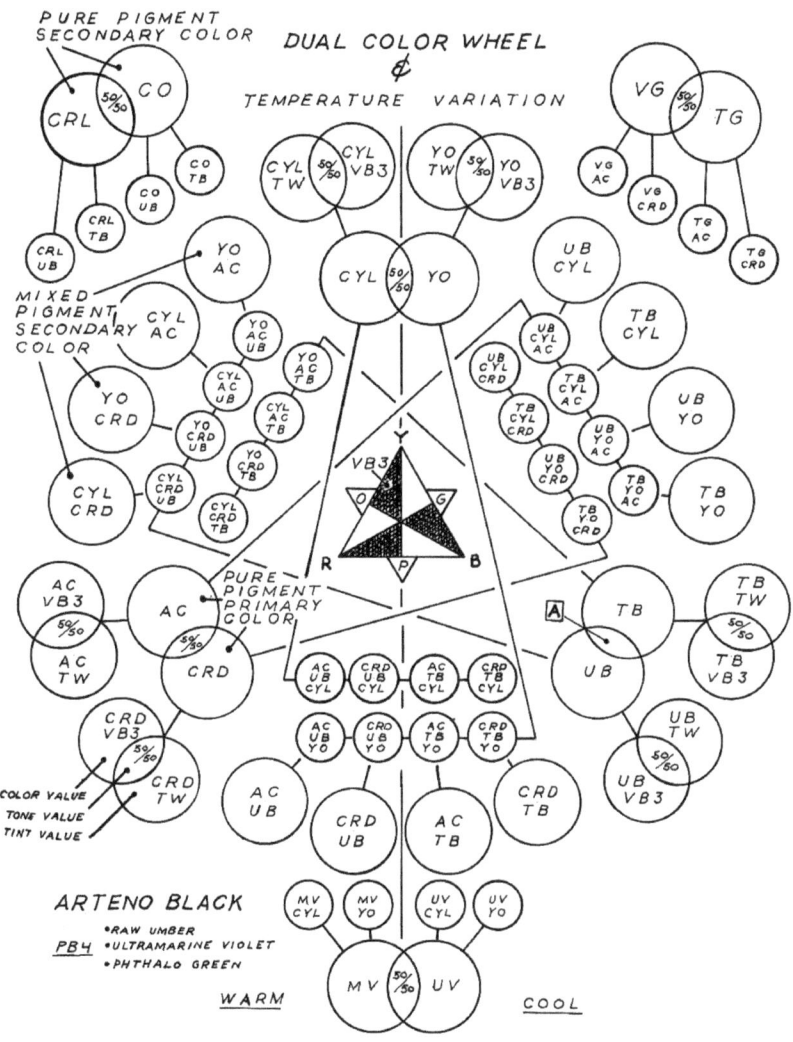

Chart 1A

juxtaposition to a color other than their complement. Here is the key: according to the advocates of the conventional color wheel, if they are mixed in controlled quantities, they can gray one or the other complement colors involved.

An observation of the 8 small circles affixed to any one of the secondary colors will reveal the grays we get when we mix in controlled quantities of the primary and secondary colors. Again we are attempting to alter the value of a color. This process is a very unreliable way of changing the value of any color, for neither a warm gray nor a cool gray can ever work effectively to alter the value or temperature of any color. As it is impossible to create an acceptable gray in this manner, a completely different approach is required to develop a truly **neutral gray**. A concept to establish such a process will be better outlined and discussed as we continue.

But first, the color wheel can be of help when one is making a subjective decision about where a color belongs in the color temperature scale. It is rather easy to realize that red and blue can be considered warm and cool respectively. By comparing two colors of the same color family, red for example, one can decide which red leans toward cool, i.e., toward blue or green, and which red leans toward warm, i.e., toward orange or yellow. We could also have two blues, one a warm blue and one a cool blue, but the moment either are compared to a different color or hue, say green for instance, both blues become a comparatively cool color. No matter which color one chooses, by using a color wheel as a matrix, one can categorize a color's temperature by mere comparison.

Please note that for those who wish to remember the color relationships regarding the color complements, just think of these popular American holidays: Red and Green for Christmas, Yellow and Purple for Easter and Blue and Orange for Halloween.

Once we have decided to venture into the realm of visual art, particularly as a painter, it soon becomes evident that it is an endeavor requiring much more effort in decision making. One of the more difficult choices to be encountered is deciding which, of the numerous different paint colors available, one shall choose to create ones own **basic palette,** and /or the reason for even developing a palette. Although many great artists are recognized by basic color selections as seen in much of their works, there are some artists who have shown little concern about a particular color choice and have displayed even less preference in any particular color scheme.

The palette presented has been developed and included as a guide in learning to manipulate each specific color, such as type and number of pigments involved, vehicles employed, light fastness, and the rating of opacity. For example, each paint tube will inform the artist if the paint is transparent, semi-transparent, or opaque. Perhaps not too important to the beginner, but that knowledge can be very important as one progresses. And although the palette depicted here can be altered at any time, one should realize it is a good way to acquire as much knowledge about a given color before introduction to a new color. See A Basic Palette Chart 2.

All the colors are displayed as a pure tube color with a portion altered with white paint, allowing us to see a more true base color.

Again color temperature is evident, as we separate the colors into warm and cool columns in our new palette. The colors in the warm column are of the strongest **tinctorial** strength. The cadmium and the phthalo colors are the strongest tinting colors. Although in the case of green, a subjective decision was made to place Phthalo Green in the cool column. And in the case of Cadmium Orange, it was also a subjective decision that a Cadmium Red Light was more of a warm orange, especially when compared to the cool Cadmium Orange. The knowledge of tinctorial strength of all the colors is a very important element of color knowledge, particularly when it comes to the mixing of colors. In the case of the two tube colors, Manganese Violet and Ultramarine Violet, both are very weak in tinctorial strength. When using these weak colors, be prepared to use quite a bit of paint, particularly when two or more color are being mixed.

In addition to the six primary colors and six secondary colors, there are four brown colors that are very important in completing our palette. The browns were briefly discussed previ-

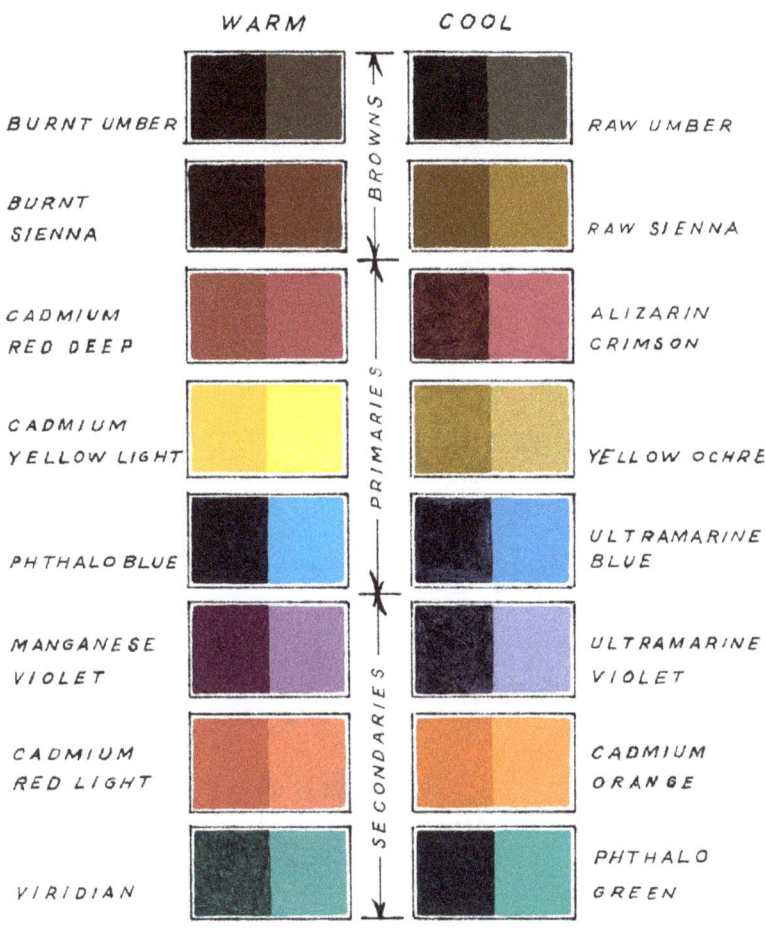

Chart 2

ously and although not considered **prismatic colors**, they are very much needed to complete the palette. Note the two browns in the cool column, Raw Umber and Raw Sienna. They are the parent browns of the two browns in the warm column, Burnt Umber and Burnt Sienna. In both cases, the "raw" browns were modified by heat, thus creating the "burnt" browns. Furthermore, as with the blacks and whites, these brown colors are also non-prismatic earth colors, and as such can vary somewhat in color and tinting power, depending on the manufacturer.

This then leaves us in need of two more non-prismatic colors, i.e., the whites and the blacks. In the case of the white, there are three different white pigments which retain their whiteness and **opacity** when ground in oil. They are Lead White, Zinc White and Titanium White.

LEAD WHITE: This white has the lowest oil absorption of all the white pigments and is noted for its opacity or covering power. It should be noted that it can be toxic and will turn black if exposed to sulfur fumes. The metallic lead is converted to a white powder by exposing sheets of lead to acetic acid vapor. After being washed, dried and ground, the white powder is ready for use as a pigment. Perhaps the best grade of white lead is known to the artists as Flake White. It is a thick heavy paint and can be used as an under-paint to develop beautiful raised highlights.

ZINC WHITE: This white is made from the

oxide powder of the metal Zinc. It requires considerably more oil for grinding than is required for Flake White. And while Flake White is adequately white, Zinc White is even whiter but less opaque. Zinc White is of a more bluish cast which gives it a cooler effect than Flake White. As with Flake White, Zinc White brushes out rather poorly and is even slower at drying.

TITANIUM WHITE: This white is very effective at displaying opacity or covering power, but the oil film it displays has a tendency to become both soft and chalky. Because of this undesirable quality, Titanium White is now generally mixed with Zinc White as much as 50 or 60 percent. Although it still retains a somewhat poor drying tendency, it is better than Zinc White alone.

The black pigments are listed as lamp black, ivory or bone black, vine or charcoal black and Mars or iron black. All the black pigments, with the exception of iron black, are a carbon black. In paint form they dry very slowly. With the exception of iron black, the black pigments are very fluffy and of extremely light weight, which has a direct bearing on the amount of oil required in grinding. It has a slowing effect on the drying time and the consistency of the paint produced.

LAMP BLACK: These pigments are considered pure carbon and are made of burning oils and fats without sufficient air to generate a clean burn. Consequently, some inferior grades can contain small amounts of greasy material.

Although the better grades are considered the most permanent of the black pigments. When mixed with white it can sometimes display a rather cool gray, but generally it can display a more neutral gray than any of the other grays.

IVORY or BONE BLACK: Ivory or bones are charred or burned to obtain a carbon pigment. But because they are of an animal source, the undesirable phosphate of lime can be a part of the refined pigment. Generally it has a brownish undertone producing a somewhat warm gray.

VINE or CHARCOAL BLACK: The charring or burning of vine clippings will produce a rather impure carbon pigment. This black paint has a bluish undertone and, when mixed with white, produces a cool or blueish gray.

MARS BLACK: Black Oxide of Iron or Ferric Oxide is the pigment used in the paint Mars Black. It is a dense, opaque, intense color and is a permanent pigment material. It is non-greasy with a somewhat brownish or warm undertone.

It is very important to note that the manufactured black paints do not always adhere to the consistency of being either a warm or a cool temperature. When one considers the manipulation of paint, this is an important aspect of the black colors and this subject will receive much greater consideration in comments to follow.

Traditionally, there have been but three general means of graying a paint color for purposes of establishing a desired **Gray Value Range**. First, there is the use of one of the basic commercial blacks just discussed. Second, one can mix together two or more dark prismatic colors. Together this can work as a means for darkening another color, but is far removed from controlling the value of the color temperature. Third, there is the concept of the **Color Complement Graying** techniques.

However, each of these three processes poses some inherent color property problems. As a general rule it stems from one of the four color properties: a lack of color temperature control. As has been discussed previously, there are four different types of black paints: Lamp Black, Ivory or Bone Black, Vine or Charcoal Black and Mars or Iron Black, that are in common use by most artists. And as we now know, none of these four black paints can be considered temperature neutral. Therefore all are very difficult to use as a means of graying any of the prismatic colors.

To modify the brilliance or chroma of any particular color with one of the black colors will often bring about a muddy appearance. In too many instances, a green, blue or brownish cast from the black paint can be introduced. Instead of altering the value of a color, we have altered the temperature of the color and made it undesirable for its intended purposes.

Although it has been the practice in many art schools to teach the Color Complement Graying Techniques, as we have discussed with the conventional color wheel, we shall soon realize the concept is flawed. The theory is, "If one wishes to gray a color, all that need be done is to mix a given color with its compliment." However, there are too many variables in this technique, making the success of the process near impossible to predict or control.

Let us now consider the Extended Secondary Colors. See Charts 3, 4 and 5.

Each of the Extended Secondary Color Charts, Purple, Orange and Green, have been developed with two different means of creating a color hue. The first eight blocks were developed by altering secondary tube colors with appropriate primary colors, thus creating new secondary colors. The next four blocks were created by manipulating two appropriate primary colors to develop new purple, orange and green secondary colors. The names of the colors, and the number above and to the side of each block, indicates the portions required to create each square of color.

Now that we have altered the hues of the secondary tube colors and created new secondary colors by mixing primary colors, it is just the beginning of knowing something about manipulating color.

With the sixteen colors we have already established in the color palette and the thirty-six additional new colors just created, we now have a total of fifty-two colors at our disposal. Each and every one of these colors can be manipulated, altered or adjusted to meet ones

EXTENDED SECONDARY COLOR: PURPLE

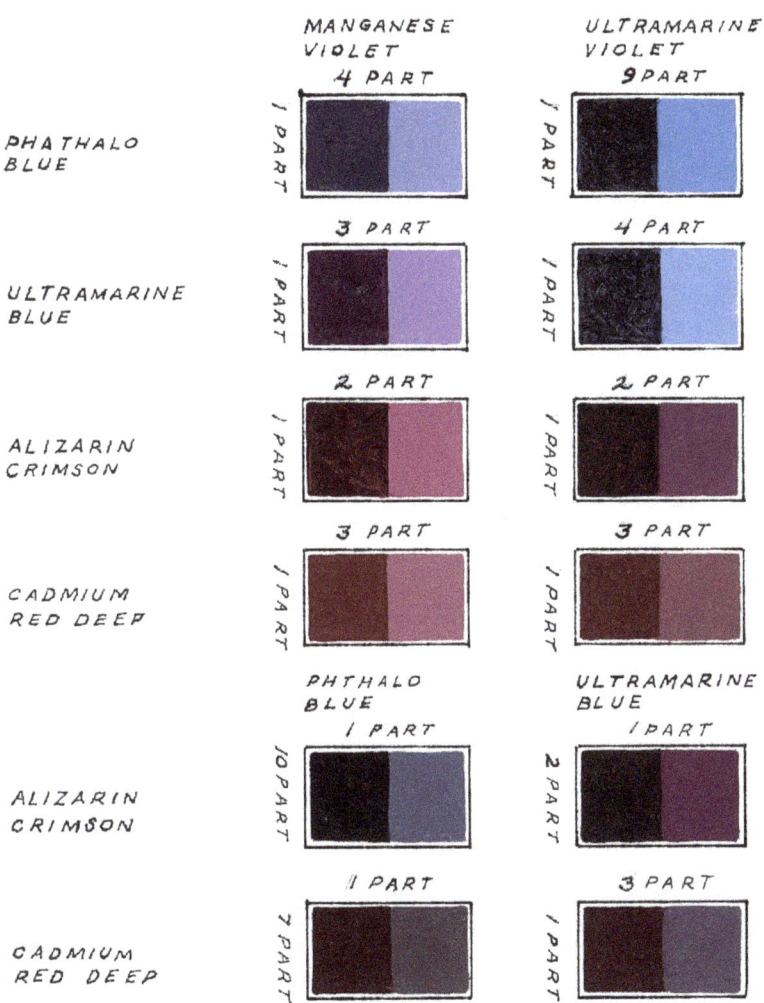

	MANGANESE VIOLET	ULTRAMARINE VIOLET

PHATHALO BLUE — 4 PART / 1 PART — 9 PART / 1 PART

ULTRAMARINE BLUE — 3 PART / 1 PART — 4 PART / 1 PART

ALIZARIN CRIMSON — 2 PART / 1 PART — 2 PART / 1 PART

CADMIUM RED DEEP — 3 PART / 1 PART — 3 PART / 1 PART

ALIZARIN CRIMSON — PHTHALO BLUE 1 PART / 10 PART — ULTRAMARINE BLUE 1 PART / 2 PART

CADMIUM RED DEEP — 1 PART / 7 PART — 3 PART / 1 PART

Chart 3

EXTENDED SECONDARY COLOR: ORANGE

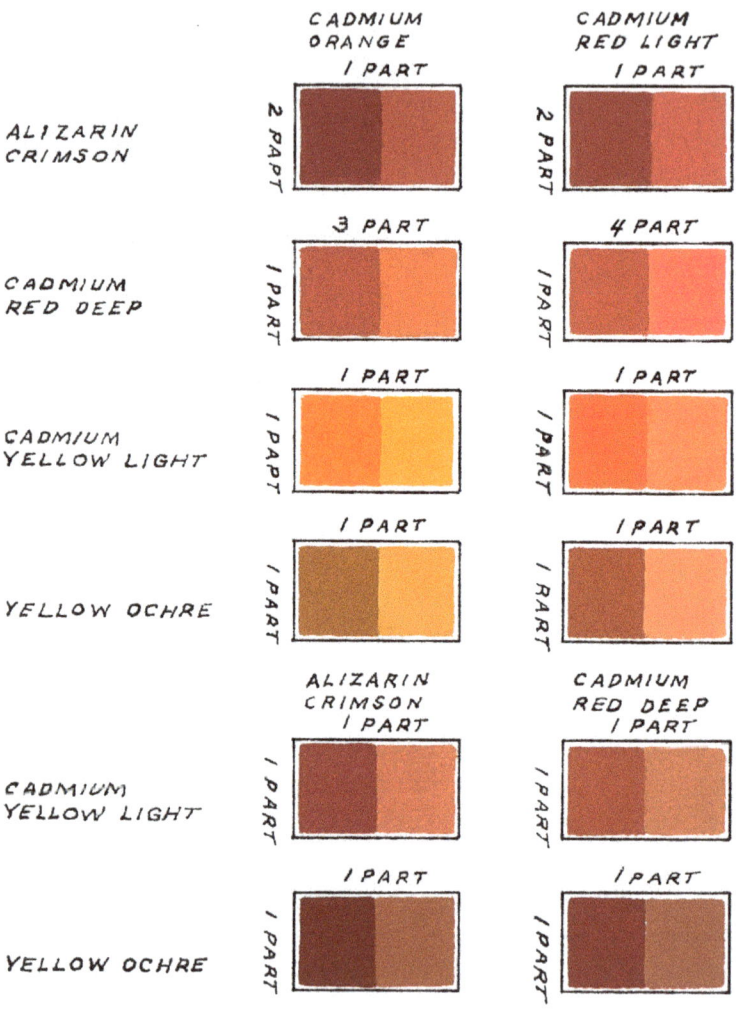

Chart 4

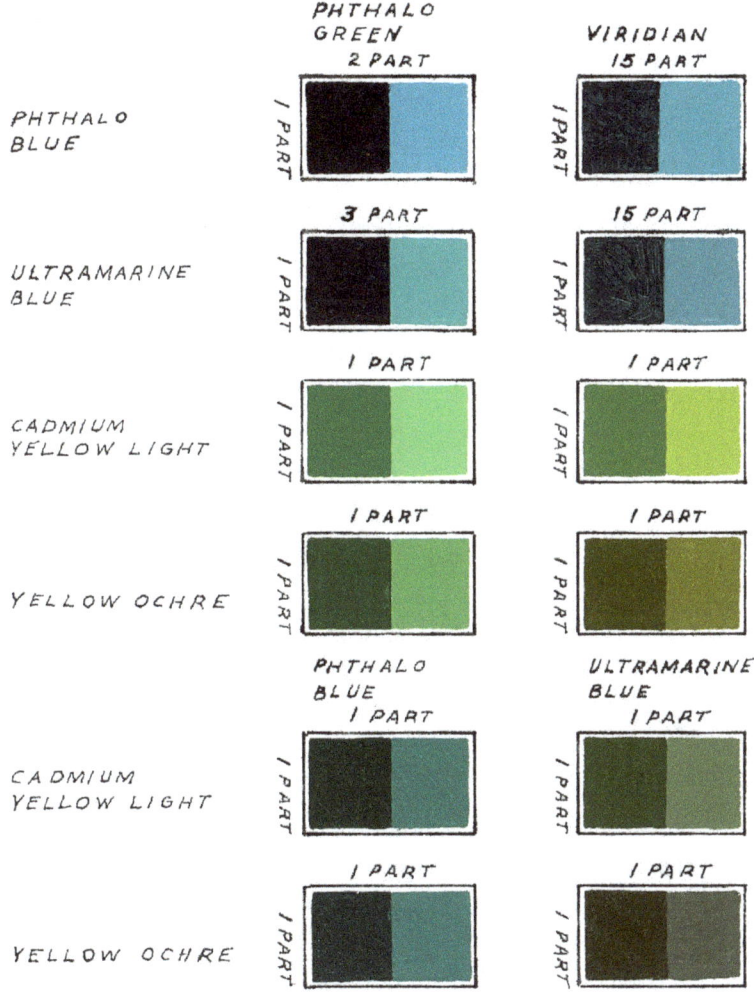

Chart 5

needs.

In addition, the following comments are an excellent lead-in to the importance of controlling value or manipulating gray. See Value Development, Chart 6.

Years ago, someone must have pondered how many shades of gray there are in existence and how many shades of gray one can control as an artist. In the mid-sixteenth century, Leonardo Da Vinci advanced the theory that no more than nine values or shades of gray are required, without the aid of line or color, to create the illusion of a three dimensional object. This concept of Leonardo's is a challenging element of color mixing value theory and it is the topic we shall now discuss.

Three Value Variation: The first question one must consider is how dark or how light one desires to establish these gray value variations. Or to state it another way, what **key** do we want to establish? This is done by developing the darkest gray paint to occupy block 1, Diagram 1. We then develop the lightest gray paint to occupy block 2. Finally, we develop the paint for block 3 by mixing equal portions of paint from block 1 and block 2 to establish the Three Value Variation.

Five Value Variation: (See Diagram 2) Assuming we have developed enough paint in the previous Three Value Variation, we can develop this Five Value Variation with a minimum of effort. Block 4 is developed by mixing equal portions of paint from blocks 1 and 3, and block

VALUE DEVELOPMENT

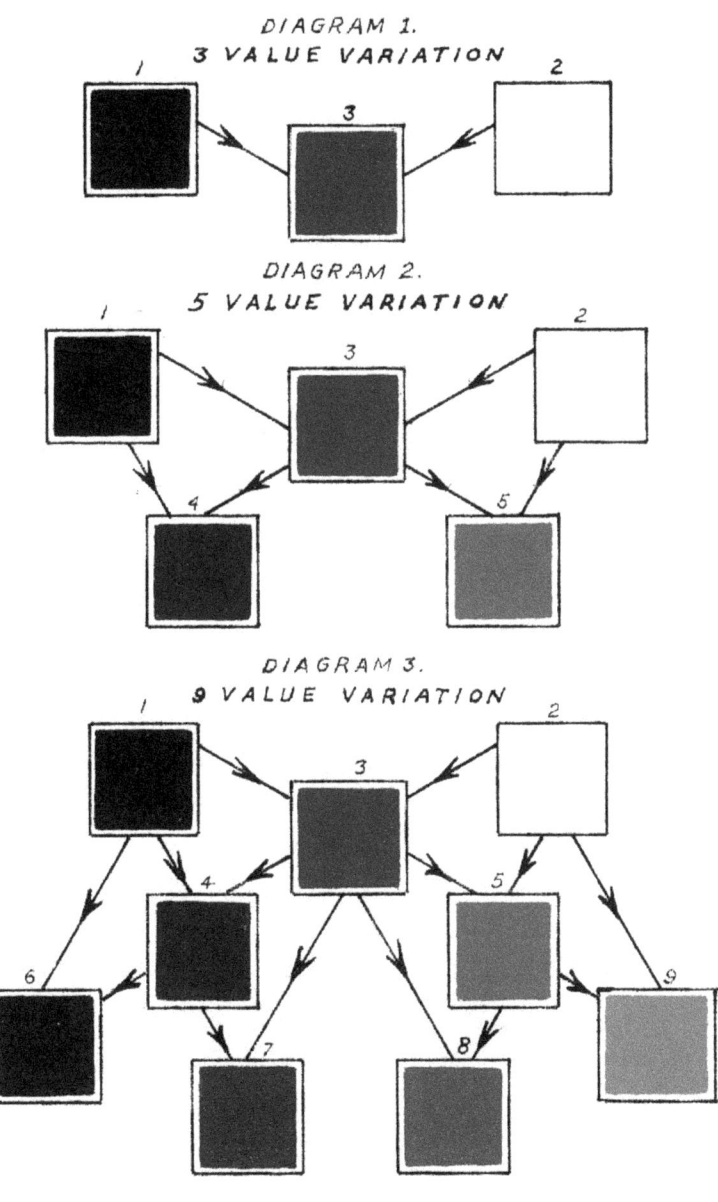

DIAGRAM 1.
3 VALUE VARIATION

DIAGRAM 2.
5 VALUE VARIATION

DIAGRAM 3.
9 VALUE VARIATION

Chart 6

5 is a mixture of equal portions of paint from blocks 2 and 3. And it should be noted, this five value concept is the most practiced process today. For the most part, a good painting can be accomplished with five different values. Remember, Da Vinci advanced the theory that no more than nine values are required to create the illusion of a 3-D image, but said nothing about the necessity of using all nine values.

Nine Value Variation: Again we duplicate the Five Value Variation and blocks 6, 7, 8, and 9 are developed in a similar manner as used in the previous example.

Now that we have outlined the procedure of the nine value development concept, let us give thought to how it can be modified to include color.

One must realize the first and most important concept should be developing the lightest color mixture, or block 2, as it will be the lightest of this particular color mixture in one's painting. After having divided the initial paint mixture into two equal parts, one part becomes block 2 while the second portion will modified with the same color to become the darkest color mixture, block 1. If one should want block 1 to be an even darker value, add the appropriate near-black to the mixture. The balance of the additional color mix concept will be accomplished as outlined in the gray color mixture process already discussed.

As stated previously, one must be concerned with the quantity of paint prepared, as it is easy to run short when borrowing from one mixture to develop a fourth and fifth mixture. It gets even worse when attempting a nine value mixture.

If one chooses to use a three value rendering, give thought to the light source, say from the right side of a geometric cylinder. We have a dark side, or number 1 mixture, a light side as number 2 mixture, and a MIDDLE GROUND as a number 3 mixture. Or, perhaps we want to use the five value procedure, where one now has two additional values, numbers 4 and 5, that can be used on the cylinder concept mentioned above, i.e. number 4 placed between numbers 1 and 3, and number 5 placed between numbers 2 and 3.

The same procedure can apply to the nine value concept, but one should realize this is the realm of Durer, Delacroix, and DaVinci, so walk lightly.

The term MIDDLE GROUND might require some explanation. When one paints, one deals with some form of light, hopefully a single source of day light, which, in turn, causes a shaded or dark side, as well as a bright or light side of any object one chooses to render. However, there is an area between the dark and light areas where the light rakes across the object and the viewer can see the unaltered color being used. That color is neither changed by the shaded dark side nor washed out by too much illumination on the light side. This is the area where one sees the true, undiluted color known as the middle ground.

But now the question remains, which black to employ?

"Art is made to disturb. Science is to reassure."
George Braque

Near-black Processing
Near-black Color Ratio
Extended Color Variation

Once this author had concluded that none of the three available methods of developing a neutral gray were very reliable or effective, it became obvious that a more dependable means or process of value control needed to be developed.

Little could be done to alter the pure black pigments or to attempt to develop new ones. In addition, the color complement gray technique of the color wheel did not easily lend itself to modification. Therefore, a new starting point had to be the "two or more dark prismatic color mixtures" if a dependable neutral black were to be developed.

A factor that further helped establish this conclusion was reinforced by a statement of James McNeill Whistler, an artist well known for his ability to work with grays. Upon being asked in an interview, "What is your secret?" Whistler pointed to a pile of black paint on his palette and replied, "That is my secret."

Could his reply have been a double meaning? Was it really one of the conventional black paints, or was it a mixture of black he had concocted. Regardless of his intent, the black paint was his secret, and that is the reason we are here: to attempt to understand that secret.

Furthermore, upon studying many original paintings, it became apparent to this author that many of the images have a distinct **tone cast.** Titian, for example, had a tendency to develop his work in an overall red tone. Winslow Homer favored a blue-green overtone, while Whistler developed a beautiful blue gray for his *Nocturne* paintings, although he was not restricted to any one tone cast preference. As illustrated in his paintings, *Arrangement in Gray and Black Number One,* of his mother, and *Arrangement in Gray and Black Number Two* of Thomas Carlyle, his overall tone casts differ. It was apparent that Whistler could shift his grays from warm to cool at will, i.e., from blue-gray to red-gray, or to green-gray, or yellow-gray with a great deal of obvious ease and perfection while maintaining the perfect key.

To this author, this aspect of Whistler's genius and versatility is interesting and requires further investigation. But why a particular black paint can be considered Whistler's secret is a moot point. It did however lead to the systematic development of the **near-black paints** that have become the basis for this writing. See Color Value Variation Charts 7, 8, and 9.

In the process of searching for a near-black color, this author concluded that certain basic qualities and properties were necessary requirements if the blacks were to be useful to the artist.

First, in keeping with the principle of the complement graying technique, it was assumed that the desired near-black must be comprised of a mixture that would include the three primary colors, red, yellow, and blue.

Second, the near-black should have the desired degree of opacity or transparency and should be of the preferred consistency and body.

Third, the near-black had to be of a neutral temperature, so as not to destroy the inherent brilliance or chroma of the color being altered in value.

To begin this search, this author started by studying the Basic Palette, where it was realized that there were three colors, one primary and two secondary colors, i.e., the blues, the purples and the greens, that qualified as being the required necessary darkest prismatic colors available. Then, to meet the requirement of opacity and body, the two darkest browns, Raw Umber and Burnt Umber, were also chosen. A careful observation of Chart 2, A Basic Palette, (page 37), should justify the colors chosen.

The break-down is as follows:

Warm	Cool
Burnt Umber	Raw Umber
Phthalo Blue	Ultramarine Blue
Viridian Green	Phthalo Green
Manganese Violet	Ultramarine Violet

These are the colors that, when combined in the appropriate quantity and at a suitable ratio, will ultimately produce a neutral near-black that consists of the required three desired primary colors, i.e., red, yellow, and blue. This is possible because the browns have both red and yellows as latent colors. The greens consist of blue and yellow, and the purples consist of blue and red colors. The two blues are of a pure primary blue color. Thus, we have fulfilled the first requirement of the neutral near-black color mixture.

Next, the second requirement of opacity and body was addressed by one or the other of the two browns being employed as a base pigment in order to achieve the desired near-black color mixture. Both the selected earth colors are inherently consistent in opacity and body.

Now that we have established the two earth colors, Raw and Burnt Umber, as base colors, we can now develop the three color categories: Blue, Green, and Purple. But there are a couple of relevant issues that must be considered.

One must first realize a "part" is meant to be a measurable amount that is consistent in quantity. This author generally used a one quarter teaspoon = 1 part measurement for most of the listed mixtures.

The next stage of the process is to determine the ratios of the colors involved in the desired mixture. The required ratios will produce a neutral black. For the sake of expediency, we shall develop the Blue Black Mixture, Number One, as shown in both the Blue Value Variations, Chart 7 and the helpful Blue Value Variations and Ratio List, Chart 10, that follows.

NEAR-BLACK MIXING PROCESS: We start by mixing two parts Raw Umber, (a yellow and red mixture), one part Phthalo Blue, (a tube blue), and two parts Alizarin Crimson, (a tube red), and thoroughly mix these together. We will then execute an extremely important part of the process: the application of the neutral white paint test. Because the tinting strength of the Phthalo Blue is so strong, even a small portion will cause the white paint to turn a defiant blue-gray.

Next, we shall add an additional one part Raw Umber and one part Alizarin Crimson to the initial mixture. By doing this we have altered the original mixture to reflect a combined total of three units of yellow, three units of red and one unit of blue. Again mix thoroughly. Test again with new clean white paint and evaluate the color temperature. It will still be somewhat cool, or blue-gray, but less so than in the first test. This mixture is blue enough that the process should be repeated for a third time. By adding one more part each of Raw Umber and Alizarin Crimson, for a final ratio mixture of four parts Raw Umber, one part Phthalo Blue, and four parts Alizarin Crimson. Mix thoroughly and re-test with fresh white paint.

NEUTRAL WHITE PAINT TEST: Once a near-black mixture has been prepared, there is an easy means of checking the mix for the neutral temperature balance required. By applying a small part of the near-black mixture on the end of ones finger, then applying it to a small quantity of white paint, will generate a gray that will indicate if the mixture leans toward warm or cool. One should be very cautious of the effect artificial lighting has on the white paint testing process. It is an extremely critical aspect of the procedure. Improper lighting is very detrimental and can cause an improper temperature evaluation of the final product, which ultimately causes difficulty in the color-graying process. If one is lucky, the necessary neutral temperature will be achieved on the first try. If not, then further correction is required. The process is discussed in the following steps.

If this mixing process was done in accordance with Mixture One of the Blue Value Variation Chart 7, an important *neutral* value near-black color will have been produced. This same process of starting the mix with two parts brown, and one part each of the other two colors involved, the thorough mixing, the temperature check with white paint, the adding of additional appropriate colors, the re-mixing

56

and the additional temperature verification, is all necessary and required in striving to obtain the neutral black desired.

A word of caution here: It should be noted that there will be times when a mixture may require a small amount of the, sometime difficult to detect, yellow or red. Rather than use the red of the applicable paints, Alizarin Crimson or Cadmium Red Deep, it is strongly suggested that the appropriate brown be used to obtain the desired red, especially when the mixture being altered is in need of increased body or opacity.

An example of just such a situation is represented by many of the mixtures detailed in the Value Variations and Ratio List, where the browns involved, both Raw Umber and Burnt Umber exceed the two parts in the ratios listed.

Further, because not all paint is manufactured with the same degree of quality, it might occasionally be necessary to alter the quantities stipulated in the Value Variations and Ratio Lists, i.e., a specific ratio of an involved mixture color could require quantity adjustments, which should be accomplished as previously mentioned.

As you will find, practice is still the best teacher. In many cases, the productive use of time is a prerequisite to success.

Consider, with the twenty-four near-black mixtures, the thirty-six extended secondary colors, and the original sixteen palette colors, we now have a total of seventy-six colors and color mixtures. Colors and mixtures which we now know how to classify, process, and manipulate with a little less fear of the dreaded Properties of Color. But really we have just begun! We shall continue by next establishing a Near-black Color Ratio Listing. See Charts 10, 11, and 12 to further our progress by discussing the layout and intent of the Color Value Variations Charts 7, 8, and 9.

The generic name and ratio of the various paints employed to create the Blue, Green, and Purple Color Value Variation chart are listed in the Near-Black Color Ratio Charts.

The three Near-Black Color Ratio Charts, each have eight near-black color displays. With each of the individual groups consisting of three temperature variations, cool, neutral, and warm. Of the Near-Black Color Ratio charts presented, numbers 1 through 4, have Raw Umber as the base color, while the other half of the chart, 5 through 8, have Burnt Umber as the base color. In keeping with the quantities and colors indicated in the Color Value Variation Charts, the neutral gray has been created and can be seen in the middle portion of the three-panel display. While the grays to the left and to the right of the three-panel display were created by adding a small portion of the appropriate warm or cool colors used to develop the neutral gray.

Another word of caution is necessary here. If one should want to alter the value of

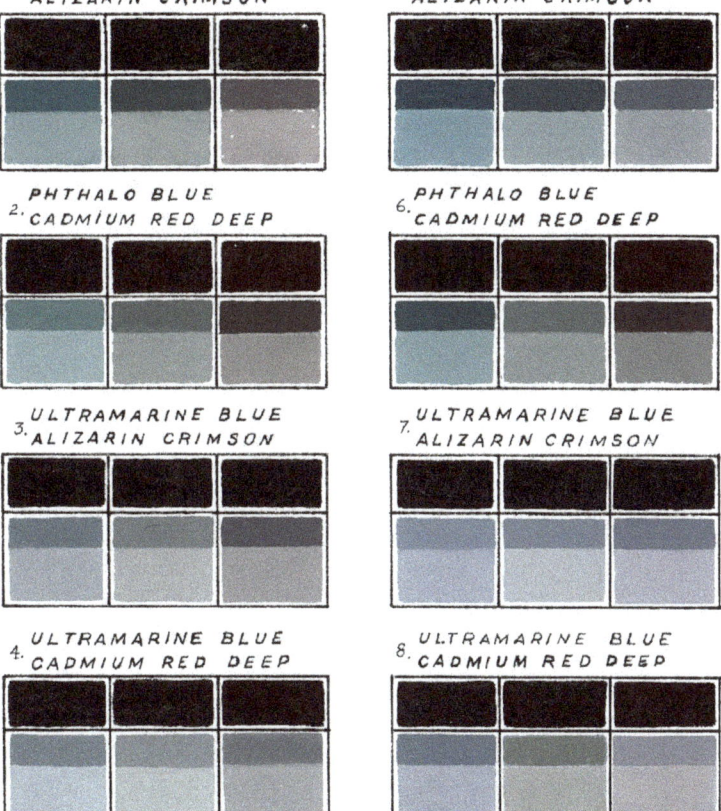

ARTENO GRAYS

BLUE VALUE VARIATIONS

RAW UMBER

BURNT UMBER

1. PHTHALO BLUE
ALIZARIN CRIMSON

5. PHTHALO BLUE
ALIZARIN CRIMSON

2. PHTHALO BLUE
CADMIUM RED DEEP

6. PHTHALO BLUE
CADMIUM RED DEEP

3. ULTRAMARINE BLUE
ALIZARIN CRIMSON

7. ULTRAMARINE BLUE
ALIZARIN CRIMSON

4. ULTRAMARINE BLUE
CADMIUM RED DEEP

8. ULTRAMARINE BLUE
CADMIUM RED DEEP

Chart 7: Arteno Grays - Blue Value Variations

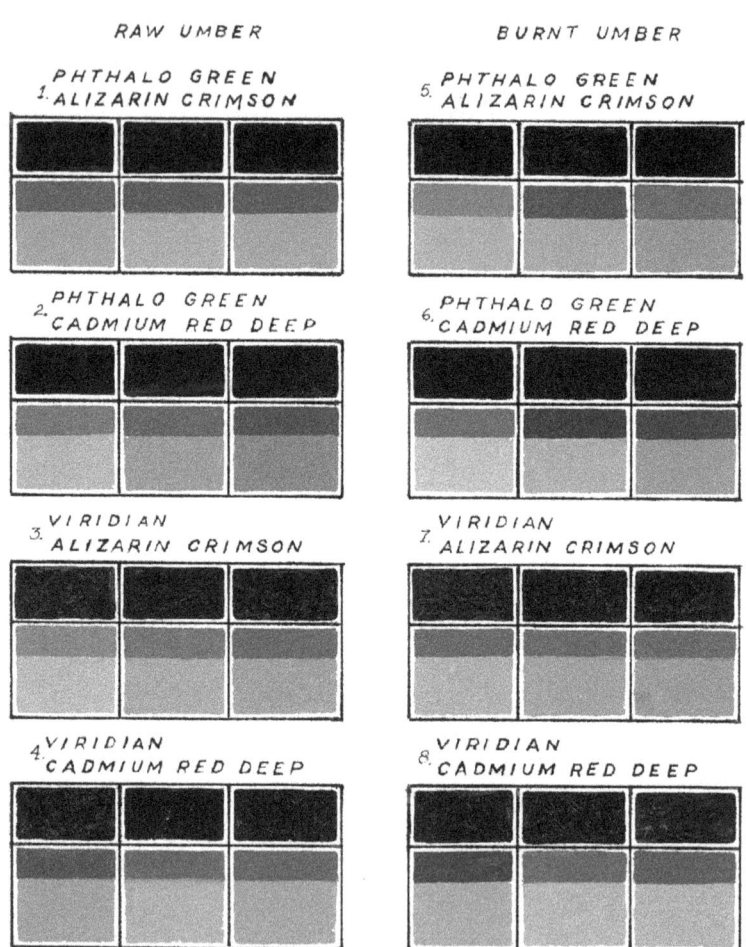

ARTENO GRAYS

GREEN VALUE VARIATIONS

RAW UMBER · BURNT UMBER

1. PHTHALO GREEN ALIZARIN CRIMSON

5. PHTHALO GREEN ALIZARIN CRIMSON

2. PHTHALO GREEN CADMIUM RED DEEP

6. PHTHALO GREEN CADMIUM RED DEEP

3. VIRIDIAN ALIZARIN CRIMSON

7. VIRIDIAN ALIZARIN CRIMSON

4. VIRIDIAN CADMIUM RED DEEP

8. VIRIDIAN CADMIUM RED DEEP

Chart 8: Arteno Grays - Green Value Variations

ARTENO GRAYS

PURPLE VALUE VARIATIONS

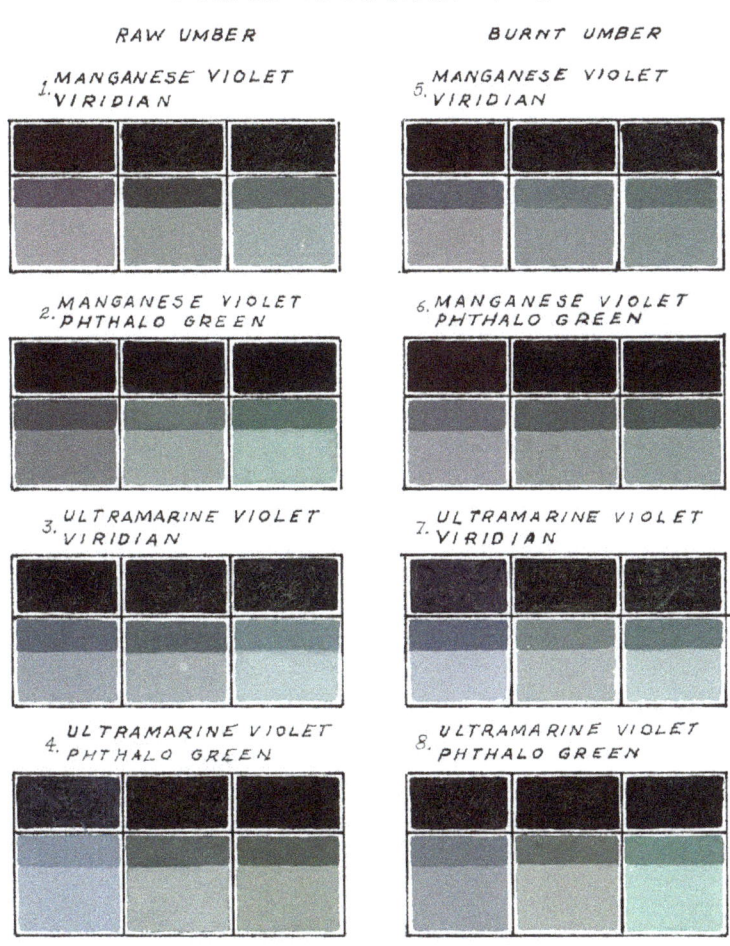

RAW UMBER

1. MANGANESE VIOLET
   VIRIDIAN

2. MANGANESE VIOLET
   PHTHALO GREEN

3. ULTRAMARINE VIOLET
   VIRIDIAN

4. ULTRAMARINE VIOLET
   PHTHALO GREEN

BURNT UMBER

5. MANGANESE VIOLET
   VIRIDIAN

6. MANGANESE VIOLET
   PHTHALO GREEN

7. ULTRAMARINE VIOLET
   VIRIDIAN

8. ULTRAMARINE VIOLET
   PHTHALO GREEN

Chart 9: Arteno Grays - Purple Value Variations

a specific color, and that color is a part of the near-black color involved, constraint in the quantity necessary of the specific color one wants to alter is necessary, for a little bit goes a long way. This is particularly important when one is attempting to critically adjust to the **key** of a painting.

The key is a term of subjective judgment concerning how dark or how light the value range is of a painting. If we were discussing the subject as a pencil drawing, the key would be predetermined in advance by pencil selection. A **low key** drawing can be accomplished by the use of a soft, dark value pencil, while a **high key** drawing requires a hard, light value pencil. Normally, drawing pencils are manufactured with nine hard pencils and nine soft pencils. This makes for considerable latitude and ease in decision making when selecting the desired key of a pencil drawing. Much is the same with painting.

Until now we have been discussing the near-black as a means of altering the key or value of a given color, but now let us consider using it as a **monochrome** approach to painting. The term itself is self explanatory, in that "mono" means one, or a single unit, and "chrome" pertains to color, and generally that single color employed can be either brown or black. This explanation is given as it might benefit the reader to think of value in terms of a single color, at least in the beginning of the value altering process. One might even attempt to develop a temperature controlled painting, wherein the neutral black is made to shift from warm to cool or vice-versa, within the painting itself. And although limited, as to the possible illustrations presented here, the potential combinations and variables that can be achieved are extensive.

The following extended color variations have been developed as a means of comparison and to illustrate a few of the many various complexities one might encounter when manipulating paint. Note that each line depicted has been developed utilizing the nine value extensions of the 3, 5, 9 value development process.

This brings us to the Extended Value Color Variations Charts 13, 14 and 15.

NEUTRAL VARIATIONS: Chart 13, Schedule 1.

Line two was developed as an all gray nine value monochrome example. It was then divided into two parts, whereby the first five dark blocks are expanded into the nine value low key of line three, while the last five lighter blocks were expanded into the nine value high key of line one.

Although not depicted, but perhaps interesting to some, if one were to combine line one and line three into an eighteen block sequence, and by selecting every other block one can develop a completely new and different set of nine value grays.

YELLOW VARIATIONS: Chart 13, Schedule 2.

One of the most difficult colors to alter is the color yellow. We start with line one as

NEAR BLACK COLOR RATIO
Blue Value Variations

No. 1
4 parts- Raw Umber
1 part-   Phthalo Blue
4 parts- Alizarin Crimson
No. 2
3 parts-Raw Umber
1 part- Phthalo Blue
4 parts-Cadmium Red Deep
No. 3
3 parts- Raw Umber
7 parts- Ultramarine Blue
1 part- Alizarin Crimson
No .4
2 parts- Raw Umber
4 parts- Ultramarine Blue
1 part- Cadmium Red Deep
No.5
5 parts- Burnt Umber
1 part- Phthalo Blue
3 parts- Alizarin Crimson
No. 6
4 parts- Burnt Umber
1 part- Phthalo Blue
3 parts- Cadmium Red Deep
No. 7
5 parts- Burnt Umber
6 parts- Ultramarine Blue
1 part- Alizarin Crimson
No. 8
3 parts- Burnt Umber
4 parts- Ultramarine Blue
1 part- Cadmium Red Deep

Chart 10

NEAR BLACK COLOR RATIO
Green Value Variations

No. 1
2 parts-Raw Umber
1 part- Phthalo Green
3 parts-Alizarin Crimson

No. 2
4 parts-Raw Umber
1 part- Phthalo Green
4 parts- Cadmium Red Deep

No. 3
2 parts- Raw Umber
8 parts-Viridian
1 part- Alizarin Crimson

No. 4
2 parts- Raw Umber
6 parts- Viridian
1 part- Cadmium Red Deep

No. 5
2 parts- Burnt Umber
1 part- Phthalo Green
2 parts- Alizarin Crimson

No. 6
2 parts- Burnt Umber
1 part- Phthalo Green
4 parts- Cadmium Red Deep

No. 7
2 parts- Burnt Umber
7 parts- Viridian
1 part- Alizarin Crimson

No. 8
2 parts- Burnt Umber
6 parts- Viridian
1 part- Cadmium Red Deep

Chart 11

NEAR BLACK COLOR RATIO
Purple Value Variations

No. 1
1 part- Raw Umber
1 part-Manganese Violet
4 parts-Viridian

No. 2
7 parts- Raw Umber
4 parts- Manganese Violet
1 part- Phthalo

No. 3
1 part- Raw Umber
4parts-Ultramarine Violet
2 parts- Viridian

No. 4
3 parts- Raw Umber
5 parts- Ultramarine Violet
1 part- Phthalo Green

No. 5
1 part- Burnt Umber
1 part- Manganese Violet
3 parts-Viridian

No. 6
6 parts- Burnt Umber
4 parts- Manganese Violet
1 part- Phthalo Green

No. 7
1 part- Burnt Umber
2 parts- Ultramarine Violet
3 parts- Viridian

No. 8
5 parts- Burnt Umber
4 parts- Ultramarine Violet
1 part- Phthalo Green

Chart 12

a controlled mixture of two colors, Cadmium Yellow Light, square A, and Titanium White, square B. Also note and compare the change of Cadmium Yellow Light in squares A and C. As we can see in line one, when one chooses a white paint as a means for altering the value of a given color, often a chalky appearance is likely to result. Consequently, using the color white to adjust a color value should be considered a definite "know no".

Here we can display the subtlety one can achieve when judiciously employing the near blacks. As was done in the Neutral Variations schedule above, the lightest five blocks of line one have been altered with Blue Value Variation, Number 1, and extended to the nine values, thus rendering line two in a lower key than in line one.

For line three, we repeat the same process but with a slight increase of the near-black, and we now have a somewhat slightly lower key than was achieved in line two. This is often necessary in the subtle policy of painting.

BLUE/RED VARIATIONS: Chart 14, Schedule 1.

This is a more complex rendering than what has been presented thus far. The colors involved are Phthalo Blue and Cadmium Red Deep, and the near-black used is Green Value Variation, Number 8, see square C. The red in the near-black is the same as the Cadmium Red Deep used in this schedule. We started this schedule by developing block 5 of line two by mixing one part Phthalo Blue, four parts Cadmium Red Deep, plus a small portion of Titanium White and the near-black, creating the dark center block. Block 1 and block 9 have been composed of the same materials with two exceptions. Block 1 is made to lean towards the color red and block 9 leans toward the color blue. Both blocks have been created in a lower gray key, thus creating line 2.

Further, line one and line three were created in the following manner. Line one, although reversed, was made by adding white to the first five blocks of line two and developing them into a nine value system. Line three was developed by adding white to the latter five blocks and extending it into nine values. So in addition to noting the strength of the red in the first line, one should also note the comparative low key aspect of the entire schedule.

BLUE/BLUE VARIATIONS: Chart 14, Schedule 2.

In keeping with our new temperature color palette, a cool Ultramarine Blue and a warm Phthalo Blue are the two primary colors of this schedule. Two different near-blacks are involved, as line two was developed with Blue Value Variation, Number 6, see square B, and line three was developed using Green Value Variation, Number 8, see square C. The first block in line one, is a simple mixture of Ultramarine Blue, Titanium White and Blue Value Variation, Number 6, while the last block is a mixture of Phthalo Blue, Titanium White and Green Value Variation, Number 8. A nine step

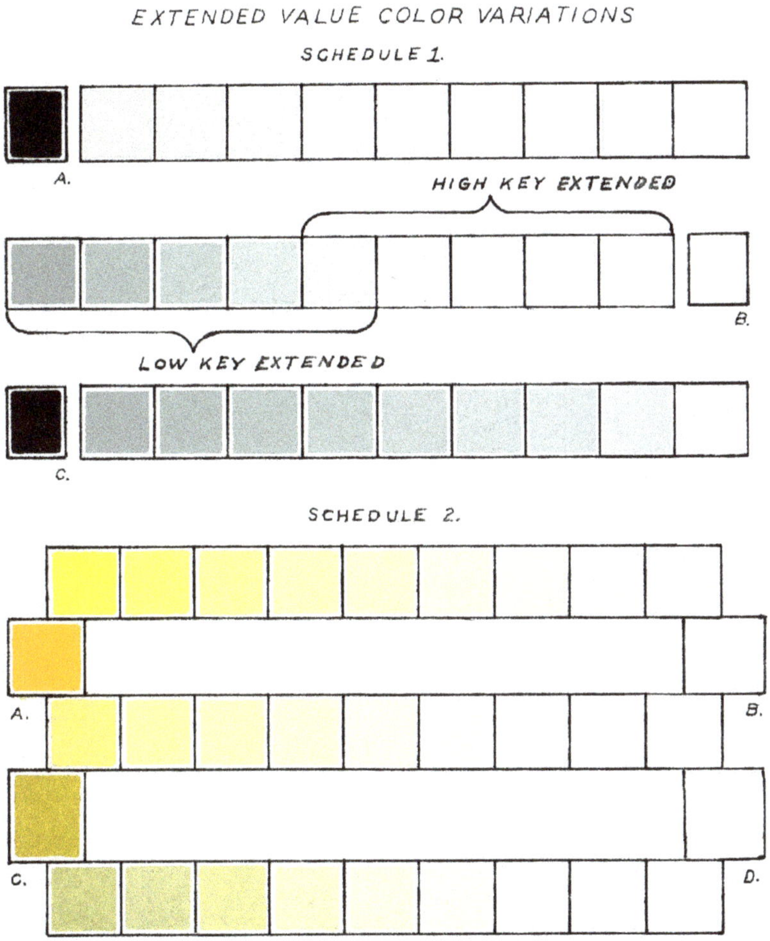

EXTENDED VALUE COLOR VARIATIONS

SCHEDULE 1.

A.

HIGH KEY EXTENDED

B.

LOW KEY EXTENDED

C.

SCHEDULE 2.

A.

B.

C.

D.

Chart 13

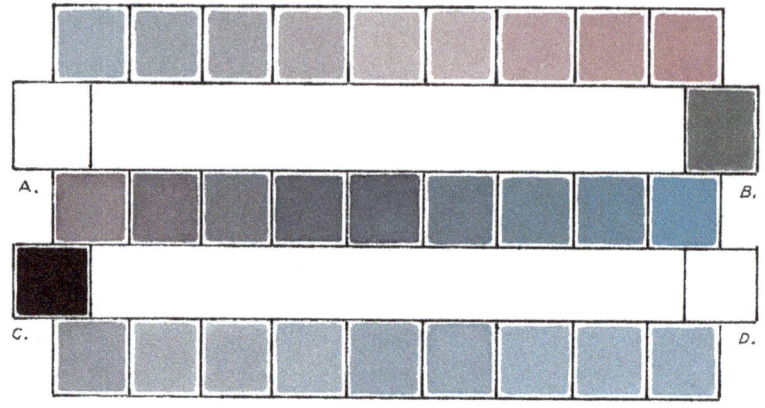

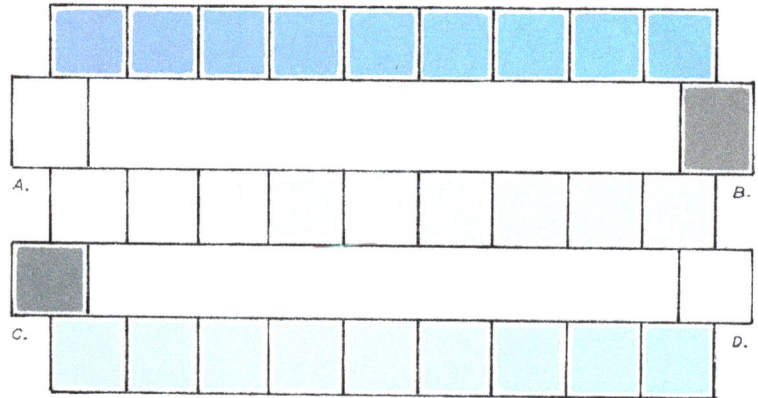

Chart 14

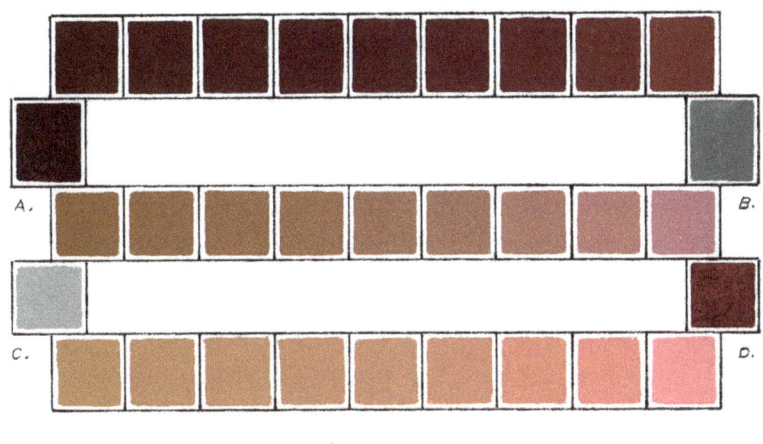

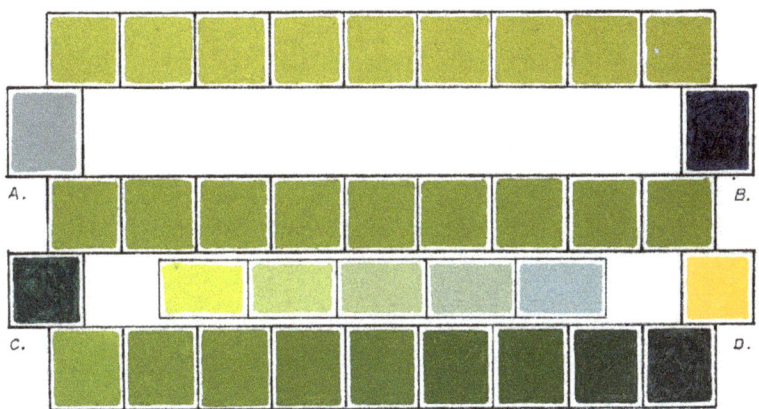

Chart 15

Value Development procedure was performed and with the tinctorial strength of Phthalo Blue we have an anticipated result. The more powerful Phthalo Blue begins to override the weaker tinting strength of the Ultramarine Blue. One should understand however, a slight adjustment to block 9 could correct this problem. By adding Titanium White to block 1 and block 5 of line one and extending to nine blocks, we have line two, and the same application to block 5 and block 9 brings about line three.

RED/RED VARIATIONS: Chart 15, Schedule 1.

We shall now once again use two colors of similar hue, although one is a brown and the other a red. A warm Burnt Sienna, square A, an opaque earth pigment, while the second color is a cool Alizarin Crimson, square D, a transparent dye pigment. The first color selected is an opaque earth pigment, while the second color is a transparent dye pigment. The black graying agent employed is Green Value Variation, Number 8. A dark and light value of the near-black is recorded in square B and square C. Rather then attempting the usual value change progression, we are about to do something very different. In an attempt to get both colors near the same value, a small portion of near-black was introduced to the Alizarin Crimson. Thus bringing two colors to a near same value and without the addition of white paint alone, the two adjusted colors of line one were developed with the nine value variations process. Keep in mind, to not override the color being altered with the addition of too large a quantity of near-black, as a small portion goes a long way. In this case we have little, if any, sequential value change. Rather, we have a much desired very close value rendering. Line two is a sequential repeat of line one, wherein only the tone value has been changed with the addition of Titanium White and a measured portion of near-black. After the appropriate nine value sequence process is completed, both temperature and colors involved remain discernible, while value alone has been effectively altered to a much higher tonal key. Further, block 1 and block 9 of line one have been altered with the addition of Titanium White to become line three. Note, because line two is of a higher key then the darker low key of line one, it now changes to a high key darker value when compared to line three which is a lighter key. Although line three is of a less gray cast than line two, it is more intense in color, and perhaps somewhat chalkier in appearance.

GREEN VARIATIONS: Chart 15, Schedule 2.

Until now, we have concerned ourselves with an example that employed only two colors to complete the illustration, whereas in this example three colors will be used . They are Ultramarine Blue, Viridian Green, and Cadmium Yellow Light, squares B, C and D, respectively. The near-black employed is Blue Value Variation, Number 1 , a lighter version of which is block A.

Before delving too deeply into the somewhat complex color aspect of this schedule, there are certain important concepts pertaining to color manipulation that fall into the need-to-know category. All of which are based on the premise that a color of a light value can be used to make a color of a dark value appear less dark in value. In other wards, a color of an inherent light value, in addition to performing other specific functions, can be used in place of white paint as a lightening agent, provided of course, that the light value color selected relates appropriately to the dark value color being altered. However, too often this is an ignored procedure.

The means normally selected to alter a color value, particularly by the novice, is to introduce a white paint to the process. As this schedule will illustrate, this is not necessarily the best, nor only available means to attain the desired effect. This is especially true when attempting to manipulate a secondary color, as opposed to a primary color.

Although this is a familiar concept to many artists, when applied it is generally limited to colors of like or similar hues. Whereas if developed to the fullest potential, it could be extended to a more complex and advantageous color manipulation. This becomes particularly apparent when one attempts to manipulate two primary colors of different hues, or when one hue of a mixture is a primary color and the other is a secondary color. Not surprisingly, both examples will be incorporated in his particular color control illustration. With this in mind, of the following four concepts, the later two are particularly pertinent.

One: A dark value primary color can be made to appear lighter in value with the addition of a light value primary color of a like hue, or;

Two: A dark value secondary color can be made to appear lighter in value with the addition of a light value secondary color of a like hue, or;

Three: A dark value primary color can be made to appear as a desired light value secondary color, with the addition of an appropriate light value primary color, or;

Four: A dark value secondary color can be made to appear as a desired light value secondary color, with the addition of an appropriate light value primary color. But the light value primary color selected as a lightening agent must, even if in theory only, be one of the two primary colors contained in the dark value secondary color being altered.

Now let us turn our attention to Chart 15, Schedule 2, line three, block 9. This is where we attempt to meet the requirements of concept number three above. The green color was developed by mixing a given quantity of the dark value primary color Ultramarine Blue, square B, with an even lesser quantity of the lighter value primary color Cadmium Yellow Light, square D, thus producing a secondary color, the very dark value green.

Let us now consider line three, block 1, where the lighter green was developed in keeping with the requirement stated in concept number four. The dark value secondary color Viridian Green, square C, was mixed with the light value primary color Cadmium Yellow Light, square D, thus producing an altered version of the secondary color green as a necessary required light value. Thus we have met the requirements of concepts three and four and have established, without the aid of white paint, two different values of a like color, one light and one dark in value.

But had it been our intent, both hues could have been made to appear either lighter or equal in value with the proper application of Cadmium Yellow Light.

Next, let us consider line one as a case in point. Line one reflects the same green hues of the just completed line three, with one exception. An additional measured quantity of Cadmium Yellow Light was used to produce a desired lighter sequence of color values. Thereby, an additional means of controlling a value has been established without using either a black or a white paint.

As we continue on, a combined means of controlling a value can also be realized in the next line. Line two reflects the same green hue depicted in line one with one exception. A near-black has been introduced in a quantity sufficient to obtain the desired results, i.e.: that of modifying both the chroma and the value of the sequential nine colors involved.

And last, but far from being insignificant, the short five block line located between the second and third line was developed strictly for comparison purposes. As it is the only line offered wherein a white paint brought about a much different value adjustment than what was just presented by the use of an appropriate prismatic color. By selecting every other block in line three and by applying white paint to each, we are now able to detect the initial colors Cadmium Yellow Light, Viridian Green, and Ultramarine Blue, used to create the original nine value sequence. Needless to say, the use of a white paint improperly can often cause much frustration and endless consternation.

With that, there is one last word concerning the use of white, or black, as a means of altering value, and it concerns striving to acquire as much knowledge or vital information about the paints with which one toils. For example, we used Cadmium Yellow Light to modify the value of Viridian, but had we used a different yellow our premise could have been compromised. For there is a company who manufactures a Cadmium Yellow Hue, using zinc white as a portion of the paint mixture. The concept of not using white paint as a means of altering the color value, with such a paint mixture, would have rendered our green schedule at fault, and thus appearances alone can be deceiving.

But then, is that not what painting is all

about? For do we not, through the medium of paint, attempt to convince the viewer that which does not exist, exists. To once again quote George Braque, "One must make a choice; a thing cannot be both true and an exact replica." So as a painter, do what you do to fool the eye, but with a degree of caution concerning the properties of color.

With that, we shall leave you with three comments that might be of some future aid.

First: It is easier to make a warm color cool, than it is to make a cool color warm.

Second: It is easier to make a dark value color lighter than it is to make a light value color darker.

Third: When a light value color and a dark value color are in juxtaposition, the edges of the light color should be made to look lighter and the edges of the dark color should be made to look darker.

Glossary

Angle Of Refraction: Unit of measurement pertaining to hardness of an object.

Alla Prima: A direct method of painting without preliminary academic preparation or drawings.

Basic Palette: Choice of primary, secondary, brown, black and white colors.

Color Compliment Graying: The controlled mixing of two compliment colors to develop a gray mixture.

Color Spectrum: The colors made to appear with the aid of a prism.

Compliment Colors: Primary and Secondary colors in compliment: Red/Green, Blue/Orange, Yellow/Purple.

Chroma: One of the four properties of color. The comparative brilliance of a particular color.

Dyes: A liquid color used to saturate a clay meant to be a pigment.

Electromagnetic Radiation Wave: An energy wave emanating from the sun.

Fade Resistance: A substance, pigment, paint or vehicle, that resists the detrimental effect of white light.

Glass Prism: An elongated triangle-shaped glass used to slow Electromagnetic Radiation Waves and expose color.

Gray Value Range: A 3, 5 or 9 value range of grays required to develop the illusion of a three dimension object.

Hue: A color or a tint. A shade or a variety of a color caused by the addition of another color.

High Key: An indication of how bright or how high or light the value or chroma.

Index of Refraction Scale: A number assigned to indicate the degree of hardness of an object or substance.

Incident Light Ray: A term indicating the measurment of a unit of white light.

Low Key: An indication of how dark or how low the value or chroma.

Light Fastness: The same as fade resistance.

Middle Ground: an area located between the light and dark sides of an object illuminated with glancing light.

Monochrome: Mono means one; chrome means color. A one color painting.

Neutral Gray: Neither warm nor cool in color temperature.

Neutral Temperature: Neither a cool nor a warm color temperature extreme.

Near-black paint: A neutral black hue derived by mixing three colors with a blue, purple or green as a base color.

Non-Prismatic: Colors undetected by the prism, i.e: Black, White and Brown.

Opacity: A measurment of how light is diffused and cannot be transmitted through an object.

Oxidation: The decomposition of a material due to the presence of oxygen.

Oxide Pigment: Pigments made from the oxidation of various materials and metals.

Primary Colors: The base colors, Red, Yellow and Blue, that cannot be made by mixing different colors together.

Properties Of Colors: Value, Temperature, Chroma, Sfumata.

Pigment: Coloring matter used in paints or watercolor.

Prismatic Color: Color derived by utilizing the prism and manipulating white light.

Resistance: The impeding, slowing, or stopping effect of light waves as exerted by one material on another.

Relative Density: The density or Specific Gravity in relation to the density of other resistant type materials.

Reflected Light Ray: A ray of white light bounces or changes direction when striking an object.

Refractive Index Number: See Index of Refraction Scale.

Secondary Color: A color, Green, Orange, or Purple, that can be made by mixing of the two appropriate primary colors.

Sfumata: One of the four properties of color. Meaning smoke, by altering a color with a lighter color, usually a white or a gray paint.

Surface Of Substance: The surface of an object undergoing refraction in order to determine its Refractive Index Number.

Surface Of Vehicle: The surface of the carrier of the pigment of paint, necessary to reflect an incident light ray.

Temperature: One of the four properties of color. A subjective decision of assigning a cool or warm temperature to a color.

Tint Mixture: A color made to appear lighter by the addition of white paint.

Tinctorial: Of or relating to color. Producing color.

Tone Cast: The amount or degree of high key or low key.

Tube Color: A given tube color whereby none of the properties of the color have been altered.

Translucent: Allowing light to pass through in a semitransparent diffused manner.

Transparent: Allowing light to pass through in an uninhibited manner.

Value: One of the four properties of color. How gray a color is as it relates to how dark the value of a paint.

Vehicle: The material used to suspend pigments in a paint form.

Visible Waves: The sun's Electomagnetic Waves are slowed and the invisible waves become visible with color.

www.ingramcontent.com/pod-product-compliance
Lightning Source LLC
Chambersburg PA
CBHW040947170526
45162CB00002B/7